IMAGES
of America

FRANKFORT

This scene, captured from the courthouse dome, overlooks the intersection of Main and Clinton Streets, offering a stunning southwestern view of a thriving Frankfort in 1884. Occupying the center foreground is the Coulter Building. The Henderson Building is on the right, and the Cohee Building is on the left. In the distance, just right of center, is the landmark "King Tut" school. The dirt streets are lined with wooden sidewalks. (Greg Miller.)

ON THE COVER: On Easter Sunday 1917, two days after the United States declared war on Germany, 3,000 Frankfort area residents convened at the Clover Leaf Railroad shops to declare their patriotism by raising Old Glory up a 100-foot flagpole that the railroad employees had erected. See pages 110 and 111 for the entire photograph. (Donna and William Huffer.)

IMAGES
of America

FRANKFORT

Janis Thornton in association with the
Clinton County Historical Society

ARCADIA
PUBLISHING

Published by Arcadia Publishing
Charleston, South Carolina

Library of Congress Control Number: 2013935758

For all general information, please contact Arcadia Publishing:
Telephone 843-853-2070
Fax 843-853-0044
E-mail sales@arcadiapublishing.com
For customer service and orders:
Toll-Free 1-888-313-2665

Visit us on the Internet at www.arcadiapublishing.com

Speaking at the August 24, 1880, Old Settlers Reunion, Frankfort's
Judge T.H. Palmer said: "When the old settlers of the county
look around them and see the vast improvements which they
have made, and see their children, their grandchildren and great-
grandchildren surrounding them, living comfortably and even
luxuriously, they may well exclaim, 'We have not lived in vain.' "
We dedicate this book to them.

CONTENTS

FOREWORD

You cannot know where you are going until you know where you have been. In Frankfort, our memories and previous generations have helped create our present and promise our future. I would not be who I am today if it were not for growing up in Frankfort and experiencing our meaningful traditions around every bend.

The coming chapters contain many examples of our community's dynamic, rich legacy. At 23, I was honored to be elected the youngest mayor in Frankfort's history. Age, however, is just a number. What you do with your years and the valuable lessons learned are what make you the person you are today.

Looking out my office window on my first day as mayor, I felt momentum and passion I had never experienced. Creating Frankfort's four cornerstones of Neighborhood Revitalization, Economic Development, Communications, and Citizen Voice, my goal is to help build on our legacy. With the assistance of every resident, we are going to put Frankfort back on the map again.

I am immersed in leading my hometown, and the dedicated residents I have looked up to since I was a boy surround me. The fruits of our labor have begun to take hold.

Now, residents and visitors are greeted by an enhanced, historic downtown that, since the fall of 2013, boasts one of the state's few downtown Ivy Tech Community College campuses. We are beautifying our neighborhoods and leveraging our world-class industrial park to secure and create not only jobs, but also great careers. We are a city on the move.

We are excelling because we believe in our city and each other once again. There is no better place to work, play, and raise a family. I hope to see you on the streets of Frankfort very soon.

—Mayor Chris McBarnes

ACKNOWLEDGMENTS

This book was a community project and was possible because of the many people who dug into their family albums and personal pictorial archives to answer a call for local, vintage photographs. Its content was driven largely by their contributions and is a testament to their generosity.

I am indebted to the Clinton County Historical Society Museum for its partnership in this project and infinitely grateful to its director, Nancy Hart, in particular, as well as Neil Conner, Donna Harmon, Joanne Robbins, and Kerry Harshbarger. I also am grateful to Grace Gouveia, Reta Williams, Jill Garrison, and Evelyn Plough of the Frankfort Community Public Library's genealogy department for their assistance. Appreciation goes to Scott Cousins and Rachel Pyle of the *Times* for their coverage of this project.

Special thanks go to the following for providing photographs and other essential contributions: Jan Bailey, Sen. Birch Bayh, Debbie Calder, Richard Campbell Jr., Connie Carlson, Jill Carroll, John Catron, Debbi Cole, Earl Cripe, Aygaen Dogar, Barbara Fausett, Carol Ann and Martin Henderson, Cranbook Academy of Art, Mayor Chris McBarnes, Frankfort Police Chief Troy Bacon, Ellen Geer, Wes Gehring, Steve Greeno, Howard C. "Buzz" Hoehn, William and Donna Huffer, Indiana Journalism Hall of Fame, Carroll Johnson, Russ Kaspar, Carla Keafer, Charity Keller, John and Vonda Kern, Dawn Layton, Jerry Leonard, Diane Lewis, Greg Miller, William Goodwin Miller, Ray Moscowitz, Donna Mosson, Ann Gordon Myers, Mary Patchett, Sam Paul, Diane and Linley Pearson, Janet Priest, JoEllen Ogle, Dorothy Pilley, Kim Ray, Ayten Rogowski, Sue Rodkey, Margaret "Pat" Rooker, Joe Root, Cheryl Royer, Alexes Marks Shuman, David Smith, Kathy Smith, Melvin Smith, Phoebe Smith, Tina Stock, Barbara Taylor, Susan Tharp, Greg Townsend, Marilyn and Willard Wilson, Dick Withrow, and my editors at Arcadia Publishing Amy Perryman and Kelsey Jones.

In most instances, sources of the photographs that appear on the following pages are noted below the photographs, while those listing no source came from the archives of the Clinton County Historical Society Museum. I regret that I could not use all the photographs submitted, but my gratitude to those submitting them is no less.

In addition, I want to thank my proofreaders and fact-checkers, who scoured the final draft of this project with an eagle's eye. They are Nancy Hart, Jill Carroll, Carroll Johnson, Kim Ray, Ray Moscowitz, and Ruth Illges.

And finally, there are two local historians who deserve everyone's unwavering gratitude for devoting their lives to the research and safekeeping of the Frankfort community's history—Helen Grove and Leroy Good. Their passion, dedication, and tireless efforts provide the shoulders upon which current and future generations of historians stand. Thank you, Helen and Leroy.

—Janis Thornton
May 2013

INTRODUCTION

Bordering two sides of Frankfort's downtown Veterans Park is an enormous mural, each side two stories high, stretching a half block long. Depicted in the giant, visual chronicle are a number of the area's key elements and historic places—a dense forest, a horse-drawn rig, a steam locomotive, and vintage businesses—along with some of the community's most notable citizens—John Pence, Verna Sharp, Everett Case, Adrian Marks, and Will Geer. The mural's many vignettes illustrate aspects of the past that contributed to Frankfort's development and helped move it toward the future. As passersby stroll alongside the larger-than-life graphic, they are transported back in time and reminded of what Frankfort, Indiana, is and how it became the modern, dynamic city it is today.

Frankfort, the seat of Clinton County, was founded in 1830, just four years after the area's first white settlers, William Clark and Nathan Kirk, penetrated the primitive, unbroken wilds and proved that men could sustain themselves off the land. Other men such as Samuel Aughe, Abner Baker, Noah Bunnell, John Douglass, Moses Fudge, David Kilgore, and brothers William, Nicholas, and John Pence soon followed.

Those early days are recorded in the minutes taken at the Old Settlers Reunions, which met annually for several years around the turn of the 20th century. Longtime resident Cicero Sims, who settled northeast of Frankfort in 1836 at the age of 14, spoke at the 1878 reunion. He told of helping his father chop down all the trees they possibly could and planting a crop of flax. When the flax was harvested, Sims said, the women spun it and wove it into cloth from which the men's shirts would be made for the next summer. At that time, he added, there was a shortage of grain in that part of the county to furnish bread. "It was very common for two or three farmers to splice teams together," he said, "and send someone or two 25 or 30 miles for bread corn."

Judge Truman Henry Palmer, who came to Frankfort in 1844 as a 16-year-old, spoke at the August 24, 1880, Old Settlers Reunion and reminisced about the time when deer, wolves, turkeys, wild cats, raccoons, and rattlesnakes were plentiful throughout the area. "I well remember how new and wild the country was then," Palmer said. "I remember the hard labor of felling trees, grubbing bushes and saplings, rolling logs and burning them, and breaking and cultivating the lands filled with stumps and green roots. I recollect how plainly we all lived, and yet how well we all enjoyed that backwoods life."

At the eighth reunion, in 1882, Aaron H. Southard told of traveling up the Whitewater River in 1830 in a flat-bottom boat loaded with supplies, hauling them over land to the headwaters of the Mississinewa River, and floating downstream. Following the Wabash River, he journeyed to Lafayette, where Abner Baker received the goods. Southard and Baker later erected a log cabin together in Jefferson. In that log hut, hanging an Indian blanket for a door, Southard and Baker lived and sold goods to the local native tribes, who brought animal skins to exchange for gunpowder, cloth, clothing, and other necessities.

Frankfort's story begins around that same time, some 30 years after the Indiana Territory was organized by an act of Congress and 14 years after Indiana became the Union's 19th state. The area that would become Frankfort was a dense, virgin forest that had been home to the Wea, Ottawa, Pottawatomie, and Miami tribes. White settlements were still scarce, scattered many miles apart, and were home base to a few brave explorers, fur trappers mainly, who scoured the rough, wooded terrain in search of game, including beaver, raccoons, mink, muskrat, and deer. But, with the steady arrival of adventurous pioneers, all of it was about to change.

The General Assembly of Indiana met in December 1829 to pass an act calling for the formation of a new county east of Tippecanoe. The act was approved January 29, 1830, and the new county was called Clinton, named for New York governor DeWitt Clinton, who had been involved in building the Wabash and Erie Canal.

The General Assembly's bill called for a board of commissioners to meet on the second Monday of May to determine where the seat of the new county would be located. Would the county seat be the town of Jefferson, or a new town built on 60 acres donated by William, Nicholas, and John Pence?

Because Jefferson was already established, some Clinton Countians wanted it to be the county seat. However, Jefferson was not centrally located, which prompted others to advocate for the county seat to be founded on the Pences' land.

Jefferson supporters argued for claiming a strip of land from the eastern side of Tippecanoe County and attaching it to Clinton County, thus moving the center of the county closer to Jefferson. In response, the county commissioners prepared a petition for the state legislature and turned it over to Jefferson businessman Abner Baker to secure signatures of the residents of the designated strip of land.

After Baker obtained the needed signatures, the petition was placed in the hands of an individual, whose name has been lost to history, who promised to deliver it to the state legislature in Indianapolis. For reasons no longer known, the petition never reached its destination, and John Pence sweetened his offer of 60 acres with an additional $100 if the commissioners would locate the county seat on his farmland. A hundred dollars was a fortune in 1830, and the commissioners gratefully accepted. Thus, the new county seat was founded, and at the Pence brothers' request, it was named Frankfort to honor their great-grandparents' home of Frankfurt-an-der-Main, Germany.

Once the new town was surveyed, the public square was cleared, along with a street on each side. In July, the county agent, William Douglass, began selling off the 60 acres in lots, and within a year, 100 lots had been sold for residential and commercial purposes. Right away, simple, wooden buildings began springing up all over town. The following year, the commissioners oversaw the construction of the county's first courthouse, and the year after that, 1832, they erected a jail. Frankfort was on its way.

The original buildings lined the streets around the square until shortly after the Civil War, when the downtown merchants, bankers, businessmen, lawyers, doctors, druggists, and saloonkeepers started replacing their buildings with two- and three-story brick structures. More people moved in; they cleared more land, and Frankfort grew. Stylish residential dwellings were constructed along the main streets, and new streets opened up new neighborhoods. Still, the city's march toward the 20th century was slow.

The pace began to quicken considerably, however, in 1870, when the first steam locomotive rolled into town, and that was the beginning of a new era for Frankfort. Within a few years, a full-fledged boom was underway, powered by the many railroad companies that formed, merged, and created interstate routes. Frankfort responded by welcoming scores of new businesses, manufacturers, and industries—all of which brought new jobs and increased services and growth.

For decades, Frankfort was an important railroad connection point and supported a roundhouse, in which locomotives could be serviced. In addition, at the turn of the 20th century, electric-powered trolleys, "interurbans," were growing in popularity because they provided fast, affordable, reliable transportation between cities. Frankfort enjoyed two interurban lines, providing north-south and east-west service.

Before the advent of highways and super-sized shopping malls, communities were self-sufficient out of necessity. Consequently, for a long time, Frankfort held its own as a bustling, multifaceted city that offered its citizens an array of products, services, spiritual nourishment, schools, entertainment, medical care, and culture. Trains rumbled through town numerous times each day, bringing passengers, goods, equipment, produce, and livestock to their destinations. Over the years, Frankfort has welcomed some of the most celebrated Americans of their time, such as Theodore Roosevelt, William Jennings Bryan, James Whitcomb Riley, Amelia Earhart, and Barry Goldwater. The city provided its sons and daughters a well-rounded education and took enormous pride in those who went on to achieve great accomplishments. The community responded when the nation called its able-bodied young men and women to war. It rejoiced when they came home, and it mourned when they did not.

Frankfort often is referred to as the "Gem City," a term of endearment that purportedly started around the turn of the century, after the first electric lights were installed downtown. It was said that when the stars shone overhead, Frankfort's glow lit up the prairie like a diamond.

Frankfort's long past is as varied as the thousands of diamonds who made it their home. Like the vignettes in the downtown mural, the 200-plus photographs in this book represent often brief, yet significant, snippets of the city's journey to today. Individually, they offer snapshots of Frankfort's history. Collectively, they reveal its heritage and its heart and soul.

Times change, but Frankfort's past is ever-present. We offer Images of America: *Frankfort* as our present to the community.

—Clinton County Historical Society Museum and Janis Thornton

One

THE FOUNDING AND POLISHING OF GEM CITY

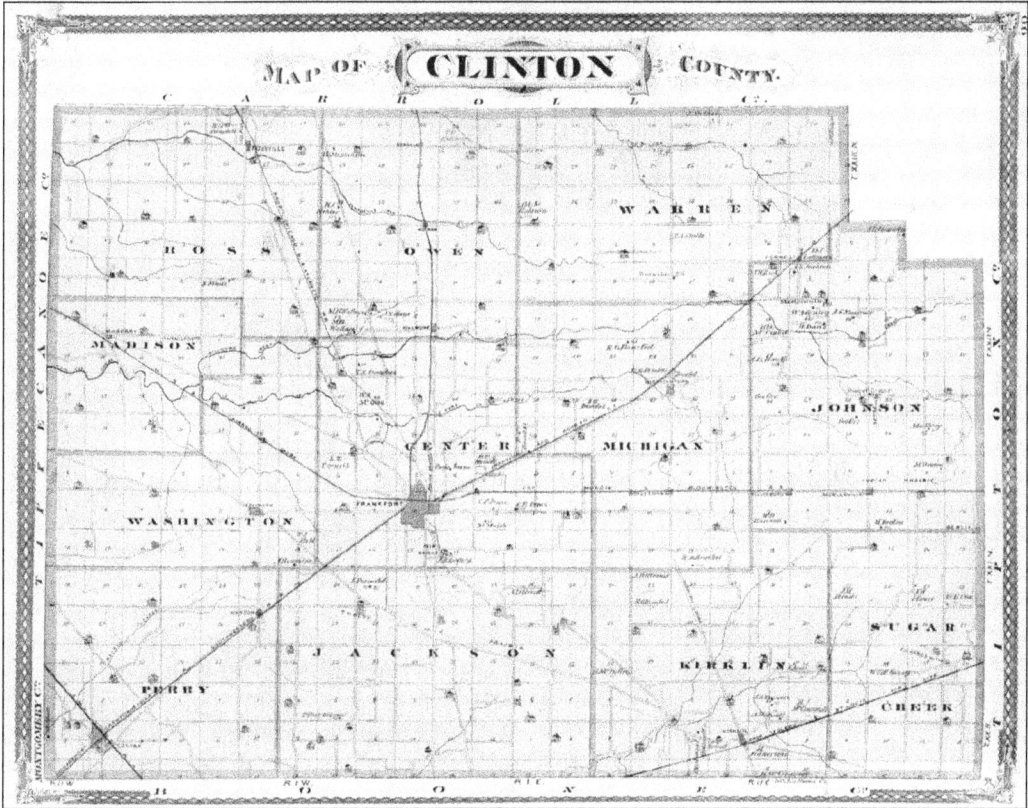

This 1876 map of Clinton County includes the townships and sections, churches, commercial buildings, roads, railroads, creeks, land owners, and more. Center Township, in which Frankfort lies, specifies the areas designated for the poor farm and the fairgrounds. The rendering provides the means for visualizing how the county has progressed and expanded. (David Rumsey Map Collection.)

John Pence was born in Virginia in 1800. At 18, he moved to Ohio and married Judith Aughe. In 1827, he, Judith, and two brothers came to Clinton County and purchased 320 acres. In 1830, when land for a county seat was needed, Pence gave 60 acres, and Frankfort was founded. Father to 11 children, Pence was the county's first treasurer, accepting an annual payment of $1.25. He died in 1882.

Abner Baker moved from Ohio to Lafayette in 1829. When he relocated to Jefferson, he purchased its two best lots for a home and a store. Shortly after, he gave the county its first wedding when he married Catherine Hood. The Bakers had 12 children but lost five of them. A successful merchant, he later turned to farming and was justice of the peace for many years. He died in 1895.

John Barner was born in 1810 in North Carolina. He grew up in Tennessee, and at age 18, he walked to Indiana. He spent time in Bloomington, Indianapolis, and Logansport, before he and his new wife, Mary, settled in Frankfort in May 1832. Two years later, Barner became postmaster, a position he held until 1849. He was elected clerk of the Clinton Circuit Court in 1843, retiring in 1850. In 1852, he was an Indiana delegate at the Democratic convention in Baltimore, which nominated Franklin Pierce for president. Barner was a member of the Clinton County Bar and Independent Order of Odd Fellows (IOOF) and was secretary of the Old Settlers Association, which he helped form. He died March 31, 1892. As his body lay in state, hundreds of mourners passed, paying their respects. Barner is buried in Frankfort's IOOF Cemetery.

Clinton County's first courthouse was a log cabin, costing $20 to build on land now occupied by Farmer's Bank. Above is the county's second courthouse, completed for $12,000 in 1838. By 1870, some in the county began pushing for a modernized centerpiece to house the county's government. After a dozen years of hot, political debate, a tax increase finally was imposed to fund a new building. At great political risk, county commissioners F.P. Bailey, Samuel Kyger, and John Pruitt retained Indianapolis architect George Bunting and construction contractor Farman & Pearce. The old building was demolished in early 1882. Below, a crowd attends the ceremonial laying of the cornerstone for the current building in September of that year. Total construction cost less than the estimated $200,000. (Below, Greg Miller.)

Frankfort's majestic centerpiece was designed by Indianapolis-based architect George Bunting, who also designed courthouses for seven other Indiana counties: Davies, Greene, Johnson, Madison, Montgomery, Union, and Wells. The Clinton and Madison County courthouses were of the same design, although Clinton's cost more, primarily because of the white Indiana oolitic limestone facing. Farman & Pearce were the builders. When the cornerstone was laid in 1882, the commissioners placed numerous items in it. Included were a copy of John Pence's deed for the land on which Frankfort was built, locally grown seeds, a dollar, local newspapers, and a Bible. Originally, concrete staircases on each side of the structure extended from the ground to a second-floor entrance, and doors to the ground level, then considered the basement, were located under each staircase. Those stairways were removed in the 1950s, and an elevator added in 1980. Additionally, the cupola was replaced in 1992, and a new dome was installed in 2000. The courthouse was listed in the National Register of Historic Places in 1978. (Margaret "Pat" Rooker.)

In 1911, Frankfort celebrated the grand opening and dedication of its 85-acre Travelers Protective Association (TPA) Park under a sizzling hot sun on the Fourth of July. With the temperature hovering around 100 degrees, the event's organizers called off the parade and encouraged attendees to proceed straight to the comfort of the park. According to the *Frankfort News*, the park was "a sea of people" walking about, patronizing the shows and amusement features. The program began at 2:00 p.m. with the audience singing "America." Ralph Cheadle, representing Post D of TPA, presented the park's shelter house to the city. Mayor O.W. Edmonds accepted the gift on behalf of the city and, in turn, presented the park to the public. Throughout the day, band concerts and free exhibitions kept the crowd entertained.

Frankfort organized its first fire department on Main Street, south of Clinton Street, around 1870. In 1896, it relocated to 54 West Clinton Street and remained there until 1968, when it moved to its current Clay Street headquarters. Above, members of the department are shown with their last horse-drawn engine, which was in use until March 1913, when it was replaced by a shiny motorized Pope Hartford fire truck, below. Although the firemen wished no harm to Frankfort residents or businesses, they were eager to test their new machine. They got their first opportunity March 8, when a fire was reported at 1300 East Clinton Street. The paper reported that the truck tore through town "like a streak of greased lightning," and the men arrived in record time. Unfortunately for them, it was a false alarm. (Above, Greg Miller; below, Leroy Good.)

Frankfort's police department formed in 1898 and was composed of, from left to right, (sitting) John Denton, Mayor Barney Irwin, and Chief George Bird (who also served as fire chief); (standing) Albert Nichols, Til Alford, Ed Miller, and Taylor Hill. Originally, the police department operated from the basement of the courthouse before moving into what is now the city building on the west side of the square in 1935. Below, members of the last department occupying the courthouse basement are, from left to right, (sitting) Basil Jacobs, Lionel Ayers, Chief Walter Cline, Mayor Dan Power, Carl Gregg, John Harris, and Charles Norman; (standing) Burdell Wayt, Garrett Cambridge, Raymond Black, Paul Stewart, E.P. Miller, Garret "Red" Nagle, and Grover Yundt. Officers patrolled the city on foot or rode bicycles until 1930, when the department bought its first patrol car. Today, the Frankfort Police Department, located in the former post office building since 1979, is composed of 30 officers. (Both, Frankfort Police Department.)

Amos "Slim" Hamilton is Frankfort's only police officer to die in the line of duty, killed by robbery suspect Clyde Jones of Goldsmith during a late-night shootout Saturday, October 12, 1929. The fateful event unfolded as Hamilton and two other officers escorted Jones to the police station for questioning. The situation turned dire when Jones got loose and fled. The officers chased him into a North Main Street alley, where Jones began shooting, fatally striking Hamilton in the face. Officers returned the gunfire, shooting blindly into the darkness and wounding Jones as he escaped to a friend's home on Rossville Avenue. Police captain George Zook responded with the entire force and numerous citizens, who surrounded the house for hours with orders to shoot to kill. Police entered the house several hours later and found Jones in bed, hiding under the covers. Jones was tried in February 1930, found guilty of first-degree murder, and sentenced to life in prison. After serving 15 years, he was released on parole. (Frankfort Police Department.)

In mid-1908, Frankfort Waterworks began digging a reservoir that was 120 feet long by 50 feet wide by 20 feet deep. Upon completion in May 1909, the reservoir was filled with a million gallons of water designated for domestic use and fire protection. The cost was about $10,000. The company also added nine miles of mains, bringing the total miles to 25, and 17 fire hydrants, to increase the number to 233.

This photograph shows Indiana state highway workers as they pave State Road 39 with cement south of Frankfort and heading north, around 1930. The tracks to the left of the road belong to the Terre Haute, Indianapolis & Eastern Traction Company.

Two

READING, WRITING, AND RAH-RAH-RAHING

Samuel Kyger devoted 46 years to education, first as a tutor and later as principal of Second Ward School, which was demolished in 1928 and replaced with a new building christened Kyger School. Kyger was born in 1858 in Frankfort. He started teaching at age 19. He joined Second Ward's administration in 1892, retiring in 1924, the year this photograph was taken. He died in 1934.

Frankfort High School's 1924–1925 basketball team gathers on the courthouse steps on March 22, 1925, one day after winning Indiana's state championship—the first of four such victories for the Hot Dogs delivered by 22-year-old coach Everett Case. From left to right are, (first row) Bob Spradling, Pete Good, Case, Wilbur Cummins, and Milford Toney; (second row) Ray Carman, John Ham, Doyle Plunkett, Rudolph Behr, manager Jim Davis, and George Schultz. Thousands turned out that day to give the team a hero's welcome. As the team arrived, the fire siren screeched, the train whistle blew, automobile horns honked, and people shouted, cheered, and clapped. Under Case, Frankfort also captured state championships in 1929, 1936, and 1939. He left Frankfort in 1941 to join the Navy. He resumed coaching at North Carolina State in 1946. (Above, Leroy Good; below, Greg Miller.)

At the end of a high school basketball-coaching career that spanned 23 years, with most of them spent in Frankfort, Everett Case had netted a legendary win-loss record of 726-75. As head coach for North Carolina State from 1946 to 1964, he racked up another impressive record that included 10 conference championships. Case was the recipient of numerous awards for his contributions to basketball. He also was inducted into several halls of fame, including the Indiana Basketball Hall of Fame, which recognized him in 1968, two years after he died in Raleigh, North Carolina, at age 65. Frankfort High School (FHS) named its sports arena in his honor. In addition to Case, eight of Frankfort's basketball athletes also have been inducted into Indiana's Basketball Hall of Fame. Case coached seven of them. The former Frankfort Hot Dogs and the years they graduated FHS are Elmer McCall (1934), Lawrence McCreary (1936), Doyal Plunkitt (1926), Robert Primmer (1930), Edward Shaver (1931), George Spradling (1922), Evan Thompson (1931), and Ralph Vaughn (1936).

The 1939 Frankfort High School basketball team brought home the fourth and final state basketball championship trophy for coach Everett Case. The school yearbook, *The Cauldron*, praised the team, calling it "well-balanced, large and brainy." Pictured are, from left to right, (sitting) Lewis Cook, James Laughner, captain Charles Johnson, Daniel Davis, and Harold Pyle; (standing) Case, James Stinson, Bill Wetzel, Ellis Good, Loren Brower, and Ernest McGill.

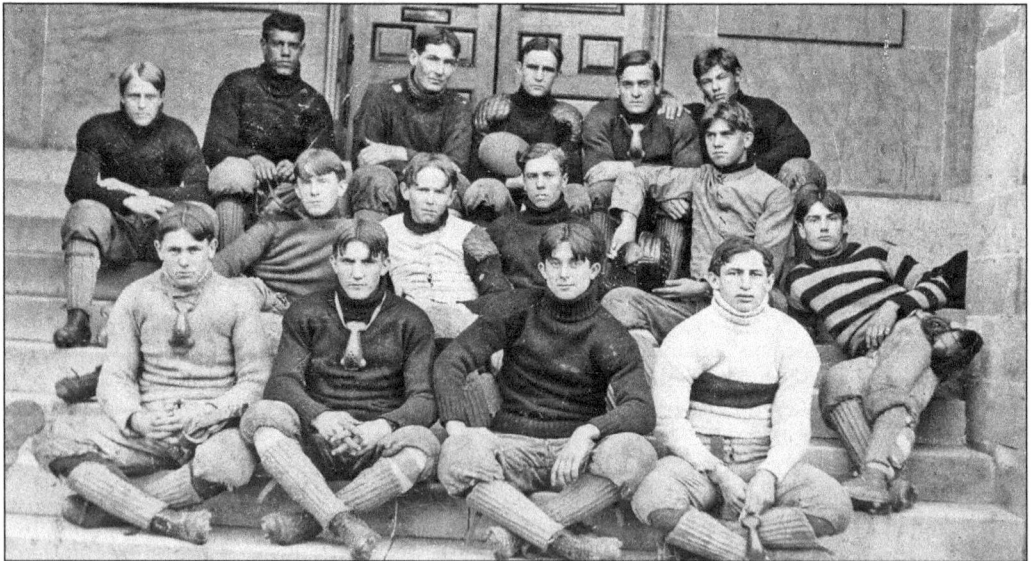

FHS also excelled on the football field. Its 1904 team carried the ball for the blue and white to many victories. Pictured are, from left to right, (first row) Ray Gaskill, Tom Petty, Milo Bolt, and Emmett Trees; (second row) Harry Fisk, Andy Cooper, Eldon Prentess, Roy Goff, and Carl "Fatty" Heaton; (third row) Harry Stotter, Roy Harper, Wood Unger, Harry Aughe, Clifford Holland, and Bernard Thompson. (Greg Miller.)

24

Frankfort Schools Superintendent E.H. Staley reported to the 1871 *Indiana School Journal* that he had personally taught 78 of the 117 teachers employed throughout Clinton County. This photograph, noted as having been taken in Frankfort shortly after the Civil War, shows the students in one of Staley's summer school classes for teachers. Staley is identified as the man seated behind the man in front holding a straw hat. (Greg Miller.)

Clinton County's 1904 township trustees pose for their official portrait. They are, from left to right, (sitting) Frank Sims, John Unger, Jacob M. Lipp, O.S. Baird, O.E. Burget, William Kelley, and John W. Amos; (standing) John W. Bell, J.H. Yost, E.D. Bunnell, J.J. Kallner, W.E. Lowman, L.C. Hodgen, C.E. Wimborough, and W.H. Irwin. In the early days of Clinton County's history, trustees served as the school board. (Leroy Good.)

Second Ward School, above, opened in 1874 at the corner of Third and Wabash Streets. This stunning new three-story school was constructed of red brick and stone and flaunted ornate towers and iron pinnacles. Its 450-seat assembly hall, 10 classrooms, and two offices could accommodate up to 600 elementary and high school students. Because of the city's growing population, the high school separated in 1892 and moved into its own newly built facilities on East Clinton Street. Second Ward School, dubbed "King Tut" by the students, was razed in 1928 to make way for Kyger School, named for Second Ward's longtime principal Samuel Kyger. Below, William Edward Daily Jr. poses with his grandmother Lydia Louisa Gasaway, around 1920, in the back yard of her south side home. King Tut rises behind them. (Below, Cheryl Royer.)

The new Frankfort High School, also known as Old Stoney, alongside Prairie Creek between Walnut and Clinton Streets, opened in 1892. In September 1922, the gymnasium, named for the school's longtime principal Katherine Howard, opened on the south side of Walnut Street. Seven months before, a fire of undetermined origin destroyed the school. Only the building's outer shell and a mass of debris remained. The Frankfort School Board, recognizing the urgent need to rebuild, acted immediately. From February to May, classes convened in various locations around town. After September, classes met in Howard Hall until the new building's dedication in January 1926. It was used until 1963, when a new school opened on Frankfort's east side. Old Stoney, listed in the National Register of Historic Places in 1979, now houses city offices. (Above, Sue Rodkey; below, Carroll Johnson.)

Frankfort High School Principal Clarence R. Young, seated at right, is credited with instituting a more diverse curriculum offering 10 distinct courses, extracurricular activities under the direction of a student council, an activity period, a social program, and standardized 60-minute class periods. Young, whose tenure extended from 1932 to 1939, also chose the school's first crest, shown at lower left. The two people in this photograph with Young are unidentified. (Sue Rodkey.)

Frankfort High School's 1938 dramatics class mounted a three-act satirical comedy, *The Big Front*, in April that year about a doctor learning to project a "big front" so he could become successful. The cast included Marilyn Fournier, George Burns, Robert Agnew, Joan Ferghuson, Phyllis Johnson, Ed Robison, John Collins, Jean Rowe, Joe O'Rear, Betty Elliot, Wanda Teegarden, Helen Garrot, Betty Mince-Moyer, and Wally Irwin.

The Frankfort High School band, organized by director Aubrey Thomas, made its debut January 28, 1926, at the dedication of the new high school. The band, dressed in blue-and-white uniforms, has subsequently provided its spirited melodies at a variety of school and community functions.

The Frankfort High School orchestra's violinists warm up for the music department's May 14, 1959, spring concert in Howard Hall. When this photograph was taken, the string section made up 50 percent of the high school's orchestra. (Janet Priest.)

Band director Aden Long conducts Frankfort High School's 1961 Blue and White Band. Long, who held a master's degree in music from Northwestern, played trumpet professionally in the 1930s. As an educator, however, he believed teaching students to appreciate music trumped training them to become professional musicians. He took over the annual Big Broadcast in 1960, setting attendance records. After 25 years at FHS, he retired in 1974. (Sue Rodkey.)

After the Indiana State Board of Health condemned the Third Ward School in 1912, the city adopted plans to build a junior high school with space allocated to the elementary school children who would have attended Third Ward. The new Central School opened for occupancy in 1915 and introduced life-skills classes, such as home economics and agriculture. It occupied land on Walnut Street south of Old Stoney. (Greg Miller.)

30

The Toy Symphony Orchestra, composed of Riley Elementary School first- and second-graders, lines up in the schoolyard for this May 10, 1927, photograph. Riley School opened in 1923 and served central Frankfort families until 2008, when the newly built Blue Ridge and Green Meadows schools opened, consolidating the student bodies of Riley, Kyger, and South Side elementary schools.

KYGER SCHOOL BUILDING
Frankfort, Indiana.
U.S.A.

Kyger School was built in 1928 to replace the razed Second Ward School building, also known as King Tut. The new school was named after former Second Ward principal Samuel Kyger. Thousands of young students were educated at Kyger before it was replaced with two new schools on Frankfort's south side in the fall of 2008. Kyger was demolished in 2009.

First Ward School's 1927 basketball team was the runner-up in the city tourney. Standing are, from left to right, coach D.F. Pitman, R. Rapp, R. Merrill, J. Donoho, E. Meneely, L. Lenon, F. King, E. Campbell, D. Dawson, and Principal O.J. Gheen. The students holding the basketball are unidentified.

Members of the First Ward School's 1927 Grade 1B pose for their class picture in the schoolyard with their teacher, Bertha Ziebarth, who is seated near the center. Carroll Johnson, who submitted this photograph, is standing in the back row, fifth from left, peeking out between two girls. (Carroll Johnson.)

32

Students at First Ward School enjoy their recess in this mid-1920s photograph. The school, located at Gentry and Paris Streets, served students who resided in the northwestern part of the city. The first First Ward School opened in 1883 but was destroyed by fire a year later. It was rebuilt and served students until 1939, when the more spacious Lincoln School replaced it. (Barbara Fausett.)

From left to right, Lottie McGuire, Katherine Eaton, and Betty Jean Allen pose with Principal L.O. McKibben on September 19, 1934, outside their Woodside School. Each of the young ladies is proudly wearing her six-pointed star badge that signifies she is a member of the school's Girls Patrol.

33

Woodside School
Frankfort, Ind.

When Frankfort annexed the area of town known as Woodside, the Woodside School became part of the city's education system. Originally located at Magnolia and Palmer Streets, Woodside School was organized in 1898 as a township school. It became a Frankfort school in September 1905. A new building was erected in 1922 on West Green Street, the site of the current Clinton County Boys and Girls Club. Below, Lena Schmollinger's first-grade class gathers outside for their class picture. Donna Mosson was a member of the class, occupying the first row, fifth from left. (Above, Greg Miller; below, Donna Mosson.)

Bertha Ziebarth's first-grade students line up on the steps at Lincoln School on September 23, 1937. Miss Ziebarth was a 1901 Frankfort High School graduate. She taught school 49 years, retiring in 1951. The only student identified is Phillip Carlson, third from the left in the second row. (Connie Carlson.)

Mary Groves Anderson taught third grade at Lincoln Elementary School. Her students remember her for reading them *The Bears of Blue River*, the story of a boy growing up in early-19th-century rural Indiana. She was born in 1894 in Clinton County and graduated from Butler University. She died in 1982 at age 87.

Martha B. Aughe's 1929–1930 first-graders gather around her for their official class picture at Lincoln School. Aughe began her teaching career in 1912 at Woodside School. She also taught at First Ward School before it was torn down and replaced by Lincoln. Aughe retired in 1955. The only student identified is Berdena Roush, third from right in the back. (Connie Carlson.)

The Lincoln School Mothersingers, consisting of mothers of Lincoln School students, performed at the school programs, school functions, and fundraisers. Any woman who enjoyed singing and performing was welcome to join. The Mothersingers specialized in popular music of the day, patriotic tunes, and hymns. Hazel Evans, standing third from left, is the director in this 1940s picture. (Jill Carroll.)

Three

BRIGHT SHINING GEMS

This iconic wall is part of the mural that lines the northwest corner of Main and Washington Streets, previously the site of the Bon Merritt Drug Store, destroyed by fire in August 1989. The city later reclaimed the corner as Veterans Park. In 1996, Frankfort Main Street retained two artists to paint a mural depicting the community's history and some of its best-known people. It was completed in 1998.

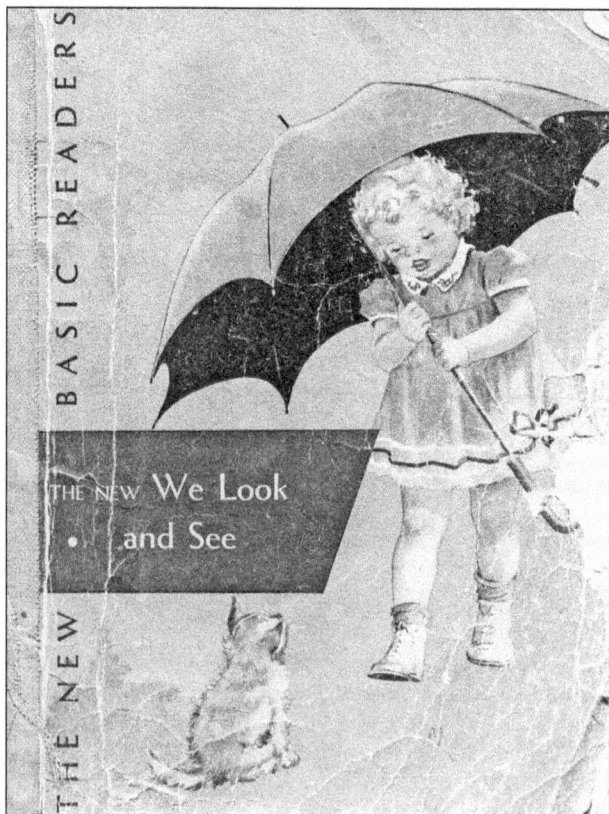

Above, Zerna Addas Sharp, creator of the Dick and Jane classic reading books, poses around 1911 with her students in Kirklin, where she launched her education career. Born in nearby Hillisburg in 1889, Sharp taught herself to read before she was five. After graduating Hillisburg High at age 16, she attended Marion Normal College, studying advanced teacher training and earning a teaching license. After teaching in Kirklin and Hillisburg, she moved to LaPorte County, where she was a teacher and principal. In 1924, Scott Foresman Publishing Company of Chicago hired her as a textbook consultant. Sharp insisted that children were expected to learn too many words too quickly, numbing their interest in reading. In 1927, the publisher asked her to create a better primer, and the Dick and Jane series was born.

Although Zerna Sharp did not write the Dick and Jane stories, she directed, critiqued, and edited them. While she sought a workable format, she listened more closely to children and noticed that they spoke in two- and three-word sentences, repeated themselves, and talked about simple things. She wanted the primers' stories to follow a similar pattern. Over time, under her direction, the series introduced readers to a third sibling, Sally; Spot, the dog; Puff, the kitten; a teddy bear named Tim; and Mother and Father. The Dick and Jane books taught millions of children to read from the 1930s through the early 1970s. Retiring in 1964, Sharp returned to Frankfort in 1978 to live the rest of her life as a resident at Wesley Manor. She remained active until her death in 1981 at the age of 91, and seemed to relish talking about her publishing days. Sharp is pictured here posing for a magazine feature around 1950.

Frankfort native Will Geer, who portrayed *The Waltons'* Grandpa Walton for six seasons, once said he found his courage to perform after his eighth-grade teacher, Flora Muller, gave him a second chance to face the class and recite the Gettysburg Address word for word. Geer recalled that if she had not made him do it, he never would have had enough confidence to be an actor. Born William Aughe Ghere in 1902, he graduated FHS in 1919 and attended the University of Chicago to study horticulture. However, in 1923, he turned down a summer job at Yellowstone and joined a theater company, making his professional acting debut at Indianapolis's Murat Theater. After college, Geer worked with several theatrical companies, including a touring production that landed on Broadway in 1928. Below, Geer performs for a radio broadcast around 1938. (Both, the Geer family.)

With the onset of the Depression, Geer headed for Southern California, where he met lifelong friends, folksingers Woody Guthrie and Burl Ives, and often performed with them in government work camps. His acting career flourished for the next two decades. However, because of his political activism, he was called to testify before the McCarthy Commission. He refused. Consequently, he was blacklisted. In response, he and his wife, actress Herta Ware, opened a theater for blacklisted performers on his Topanga, California, property. Years later, they formed Theatricum Botanicum, a nonprofit corporation. Over his career, Geer starred in numerous film and television productions, ending with *The Waltons*. Frankfort gave him a warm welcome when he returned for Will Geer Days (right) in 1976. He died in 1978. Above, he poses with his young family at their home. (Above, the Geer family.)

Before teaching music in Clinton County, Frankfort native Freddie Shaffer played trumpet with Fred Waring and Paul Whiteman. In 1938, he picked 15 talented young women, many of them teenagers, and formed a band. By 1941, Shaffer's group was performing throughout Indiana at clubs and lodges weekends only. In 1942, that changed when Shaffer accepted a weeklong job at Geneva-on-the-Lake, Ohio. The band was a hit and stayed all summer. With World War II in full swing, the band became known as the Victory Sweethearts and toured the United States, performing at a variety of venues, including USOs and military bases. After the war, however, the girls began marrying and going their own way. Shaffer reluctantly dissolved the group in 1953 and returned to Frankfort, where he died three years later at age 53. Below, the band poses in Galveston, Texas.

Clinton County's Gerald "Curley" Myers started his career at age nine performing at area social gatherings. After high school, Myers formed the Hoosier Ramblers, regulars on WDAN radio in Danville, Illinois. They later moved to WLW in Cincinnati and changed their name to the Buccaneers. Early in 1955, Indianapolis-based WFBM-TV started airing *Indiana Hoedown*, featuring the WLW stars. Myers alo starred in *Curley's Cowboy Theater* for eight years and then a Saturday morning kids' show with cohosts and friends Jerry Vance and Hal Fryer. After WFBM-TV was sold in 1972, Myers continued to perform throughout Central Indiana for many years. He died in May 2013. At right, Myers and his daughter Vickie chat with NBC's *Bonanza* stars, Lorne Greene and Dan Blocker, during a WFBM-TV broadcast in 1962.

Charles Aidman had one of those faces that is familiar but a little hard to place. Aidman was born in Frankfort in 1925 and graduated FHS in 1943. After college and a Navy stint, he studied acting and became one of Hollywood's most accomplished character actors, working in films such as *Pork Chop Hill* and *Kotch* and guest-starring in several television shows. He died in Beverly Hills in 1993. (The David L. Smith Collection.)

Frankfort-born film and television actor Anthony Caruso was 10 when his family moved to Long Beach, California, in 1926. While studying acting at the Pasadena Playhouse, he befriended Alan Ladd, with whom he would later work on 11 films. Caruso made his screen debut in 1939 portraying a villain, and stuck with that persona throughout his career. Caruso died in Brentwood, California, in 2003. (The David L. Smith Collection.)

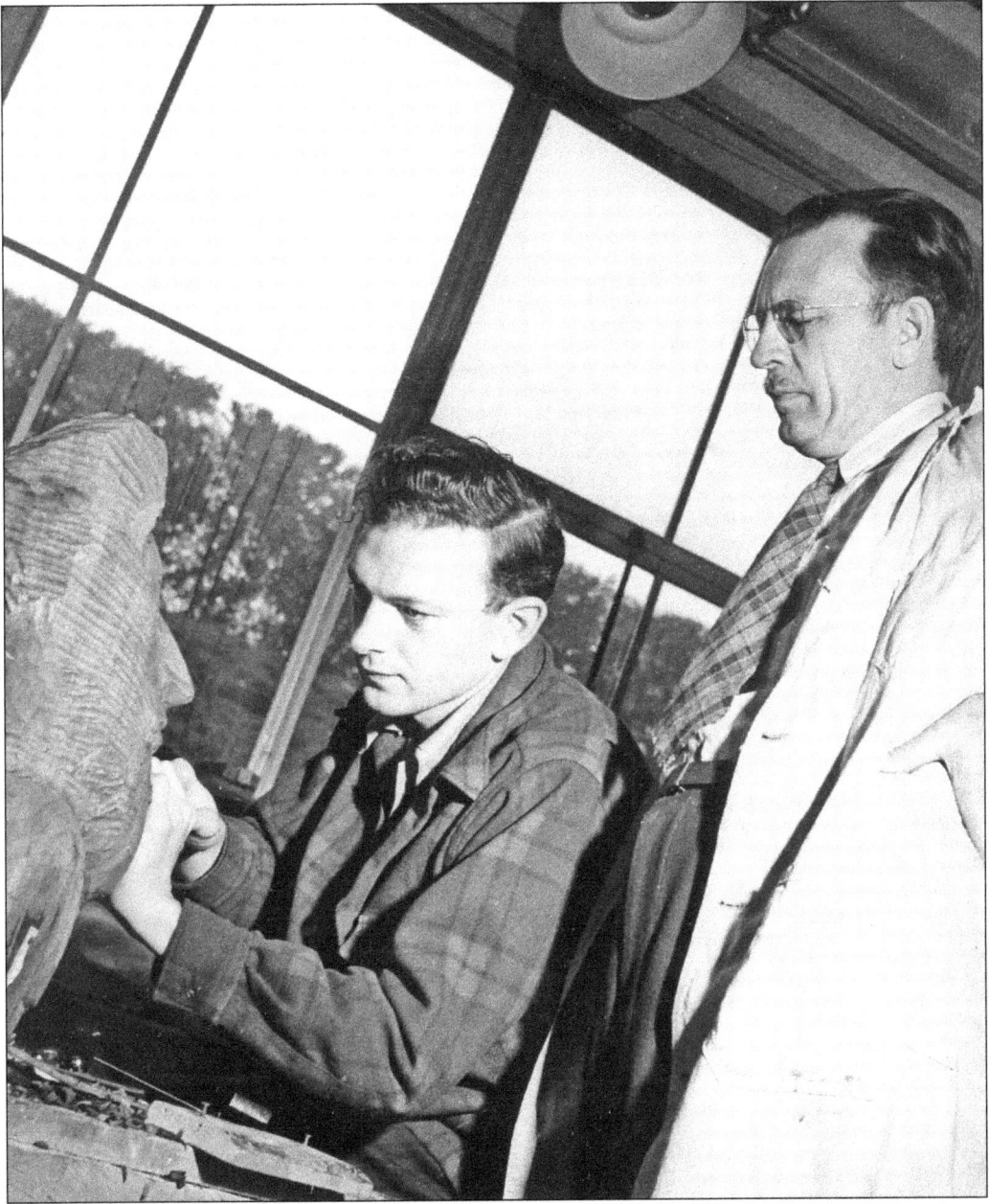

Sculptor Jon Magnus Jonson, right, works with a student at his studio at the Cranbrook Academy of Art in Bloomfield Hills, Michigan, where he taught from 1944 to 1947. Jonson was born in 1893 near Upham, North Dakota, to Icelandic immigrant parents. After his World War I military service, he attended art schools in Chicago and New York, eventually joining the faculty at Cranbrook Academy of Art. Jonson married Lela Maish of Frankfort and maintained a farmhouse in the Frankfort area for many years. Among his many works are the fountain at Frankfort's TPA Park and three sculptures located outside Purdue University's Elliott Hall of Music in West Lafayette, Indiana. The printed program for a 1947 memorial exhibition described Jonson as "a subtle combination of self-effacement, inner discipline and passion." He died of a heart attack in 1947. He was 53. (The Cranbrook Academy of Art.)

Newly elected Clinton County treasurer Lucille Wooffendale, left, is sworn into office by Beth Conrad, Clinton Circuit Court reporter, on January 2, 1951. Wooffendale had numerous achievements throughout her career, and many people considered her a trailblazer for women in politics and business. In 1950, she became the county's first female elected to a political office. While serving two terms as county clerk, the State Clerks Association named her Outstanding Clerk in 1970. In 1972, she was elected state representative for the 28th District. Wooffendale also was a founder of the Frankfort Zonta Club and was appointed to numerous community service boards.

Lucille was one of 10 McEwen children, eight of them daughters. Pictured around 1945, they are, from left to right, Rosemary, Mary Ann, Lucille, Jane, Margaret, Betty, Martha, and Janie. Lucille Wooffendale died in 1991. (Barbara Fausett.)

Frankfort defense attorney Frank Pryor, standing, was involved in many high-profile cases, union issues, and politics. Here, he poses with then-Indiana state representative (and future US senator) Birch Bayh, left, and then-Indiana governor Harold Handley, second from left, at a dinner around 1958. During his nearly 60-year career, Pryor acquired an almost legendary reputation for his masterful courtroom presence. Perhaps his most famous case was his 1950 defense of Frankie Miller, a Frankfort woman who confessed to killing her lover with a shotgun blast. During the trial, Pryor painted Miller as a victim. The jury found her guilty of manslaughter, for which she served a two-year prison sentence. Then-Clinton County sheriff Maynard Lewis, right, arrested Miller. Lewis and his family lived in a house attached to the jail, which, at the time, was located on Washington Street. (Right, Diane Lewis.)

Frankfort's Linley Pearson, surrounded by, from left to right, his daughter Shelley, wife Diane, and daughter Nikki, waves on primary election night, May 5, 1992, upon learning he was the Republican gubernatorial candidate, running against incumbent Democrat Evan Bayh. Previously, Pearson was Clinton County prosecutor for 10 years and Indiana attorney general for 12 years. In 1994, he was elected Clinton Circuit Court judge and served until retiring in 2012. (Linley and Diane Pearson.)

Rana Foroohar, who grew up in Frankfort, is *Time* magazine's assistant managing editor in charge of economics and business. She also broadcasts a weekly radio show on WNYC and frequently is a guest commentator for CBS, NBC, MSNBC, CNN, BBC, and NPR on economic, political, and foreign affairs. She is a graduate of Frankfort High School, Barnard College, and Columbia University. (Aygen Dogar.)

Four

NEIGHBORS AND FRIENDS

Frankfort's friendly mail carriers pose for this early 1950s photograph outside the post office, then located at Columbia and Washington Streets. The men are identified as, from left to right, (kneeling) Bob Eaton, Emerson Cornelison, Argyle Hutchison, Calvin Gwinn, John Clark, and Joseph Daywitt; (standing) John Layton, Jim Ostler, Henry Gillespie, Earnest Peters, Franklin Isgrigg, Herbert Baker, and M. Smith.

Two-year-old Leroy Good wears his favorite suit in this 1922 photograph. He was born in the first house west of Bunnell Cemetery and has since lived in five houses, all within a mile. He graduated from Jefferson High School in 1937 and entered the Army in 1942. After the war, he worked for the Jefferson elevator for 35 years. Today, he is one of Clinton County's favorite historians. (Leroy Good.)

Margaret "Pat" Rooker, age four, smiles sweetly, although she claims today that, as a child, she was a tomboy. The daughter of Zula and T.O. Wade, she grew up in Frankfort, graduating high school in 1937. She married the Rev. Robert Rooker in 1941 and spent almost 69 years with him ministering to several congregations, including Geetingsville Presbyterian Church. (Margaret "Pat" Rooker.)

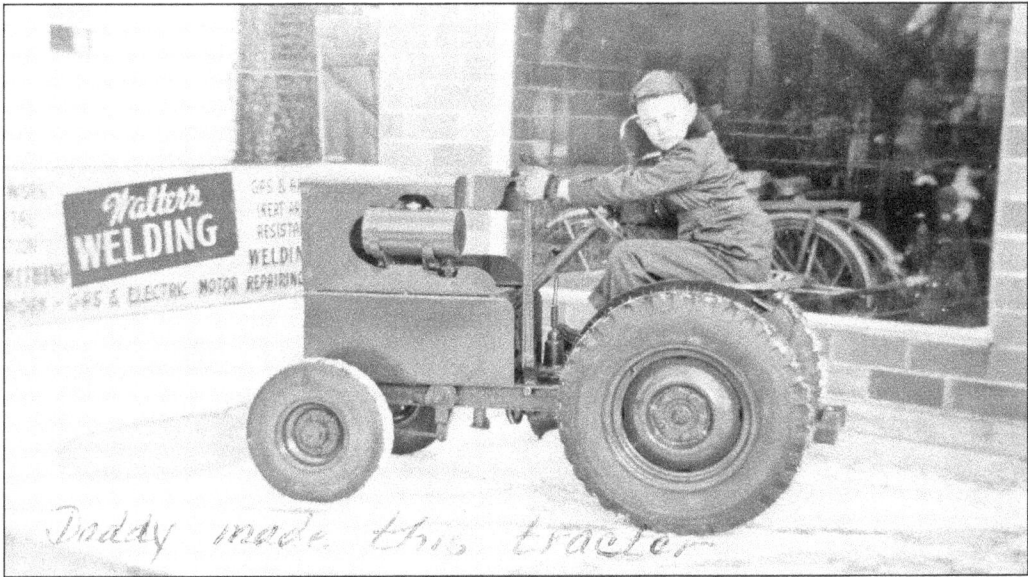

Daddy made this tractor

Johnny Walters was the beneficiary of many of the inventions created by his father, Honk. Here, he rides the miniature tractor his dad made for him in 1952. Walters graduated Frankfort High School in 1959 and worked for National Cigar Company all his adult life. He died in 2003. (Barbara Fausett.)

Vessie Berle Alter graduated from Indiana University around 1908 and taught school in Forest Township until she married Theodore Carl Merrick 10 years later. In those days, schools rarely employed married women as teachers, so she had to choose between marriage and career. The Merricks lived in Forest Township all their lives and raised two children, Maxine and Carl Wayne. Vessie died in 1978. (Phoebe Smith.)

Above, Frankfort resident Ed McIlrath, a Clover Leaf railroad car repairman, poses at the intersection of South Third and West South Streets, ready to ride in the 1915 Red Men's Parade. The Order of Red Men originally organized during the buildup to the Revolutionary War, and its members participated in the 1773 Boston Tea Party. Over the ensuing years, the group transformed into the Odd Fellows. Locally, the Odd Fellows organization occupied the second floor of the building on the northeast corner of Jackson and Clinton Streets for many years. Below, members of the local Dakota Tribe of the Improved Order of Red Men line up outside the courthouse.

The Goodwin family posed for this portrait around 1900. Pictured are, from left to right, (sitting) Goodwin Furniture and Undertaking founder George William Goodwin (who also served as a justice of the peace and a Frankfort School Board member), John Charles Goodwin, and Elizabeth Shortle Goodwin; (standing) James Samuel Goodwin, William Henry Goodwin, and Alice Goodwin. Goodwin Funeral Home has served the Frankfort community since 1856. (William Goodwin Miller.)

From left to right are Ida Mae Ramey, unidentified, and Ray, Roy, and William Ramey at their home at 1256 West McClurg Street. Ray and Roy operated Ramey Bros. Burial Vault Company at this location for many years. (Donna and William Huffer.)

Zula Martin graduated Frankfort High School around 1907 and relocated to North Dakota, where she taught in a one-room school. Enduring two hard winters, she returned home to attend business school. Afterward, she kept books for a railroad office until 1911, when she married Thurl O. Wade. After his death in 1933, Zula ran his plumbing, heating, and well-drilling business. She lived to the age of 99. (Margaret "Pat" Rooker.)

Zula Martin's mother, Margaret "Maggie" Martin, was born in 1860 on the Ten-Mile Prairie, southeast of Frankfort. She married John Martin, a house painter, in 1879. John fell from scaffolding and died in 1889, leaving Maggie to raise their three children. Maggie took in sewing and made hats, later working 23 years in the millinery departments at F.B. Cohee's Dry Goods and Thrasher's Department Store. (Margaret "Pat" Rooker.)

George T. Dinwiddie was an honorary colonel of the executive staff for Indiana governor James Goodrich (1917–1921) and was elected to two terms as chairman of the Indiana Republican Party. Professionally, he was involved with banking and finance. Early in his career, he owned a hardware store on the square with partner John H. Coulter and later with James P. Gaddis. Dinwiddie died in 1933 at age 78.

Members of the Campbell and Barnett families gather in Frankfort in 1914 for the wedding of John Barnett and Minnie Jane Moore. Pictured are, from left tot right, (first row) Carlotta Barnett, John Westly Barnett, John W. Campbell (baby), John Moore, and Nancy Moore; (second row) John Jasper Campbell, Clarence Campbell, Grace Campbell, John David Barnett, and Minnie Jane Moore Barnett. (Richard Campbell Jr.)

Murl Stevenson Maish, son William Mordecau, and wife, Audra Opal Huffer Maish, pose for a family portrait around 1920. Murl Maish was a farmer in Johnson Township. He and his wife belonged to the Hillisburg Methodist Church. In addition to Bill, they also had a daughter, Dorothy, and an infant, who died. (Phoebe Smith.)

The Bill Maish family, photographed in 1952, lived on a farm in Johnson Township near Clinton Central High School. Members are, from left to right, (first row) Glenda and Phoebe; (second row) Judy and Ralph; (third row) Maxine and Bill Maish. (Phoebe Smith.)

Ralph (left) and Carl Stinson—The Stinson Brothers—were popular performers throughout Clinton County in the 1930s and 1940s. Ralph was appointed deputy sheriff by Clinton County sheriff Maynard Lewis in the late 1940s and served as sheriff from 1959 to 1967. He died in 1977. Carl was a barber at the Roxy Barbershop and taught music. In 1972, he retired to Bloomington, where he died in 1983.

Versatile handyman Commodore "Honk" Walters owned Walters Welding Shop in Frankfort from 1947 to 1983. He also was a carman for the Nickel Plate Railroad for 43 years. Walters was an enterprising inventor and craftsman, producing miniature cars and tractors, motorcycles, decorative flower stands, wood splitters, and more. Born in Frankfort in 1906, he and wife Naomi raised six children. He died in 1999. (Barbara Fausett.)

Home economics clubs began forming in Clinton County in 1921 to encourage members to further their homemaking education through the Home Extension Service of Purdue University. Two leaders from each township met monthly with an instructor, who taught homemaking techniques such as canning, cooking, and sewing. The leaders then shared the lessons with members of their township club. Bernice Boggs Humrickhouse of Frankfort (pictured) was the first county club president. (Clinton County Extension Office.)

By 1936, Clinton County had 17 active home economics clubs, supported by approximately 660 members. The county officers, the 17 club presidents, and the scrapbook committee gather for this photograph at their January 1936 meeting in rural Frankfort. (Clinton County Extension Office.)

Center Township's Home Economics Club officers for 1936 were, from left to right, Mrs. Frank Culbertson, president; Mrs. Ralph Pyles, vice president; Mrs. Ralph Reed, secretary; and Mrs. Easdale Pickett, treasurer. The Extension Homemakers Club is still active today, providing its members with opportunities for education, personal growth, and altruistic outreach. (Clinton County Extension Office.)

Members of First Christian Church's Priscilla Embroidery Club gathered around 1910. They are, from left to right, (first row) Jessie Ruddell Fennel and Fannie Ruddell Shanklin; (second row) Lennie Miller, Bertha Newby Fisher, Sarah Ruddell Sims, Mrs. Will Shanklin, Mrs. Dorty, Mrs. Sylvester Kintz, Edith Beardsley Cromwell, Martha Wallace, and Mrs. Hillis; (third row) Mrs. Ed Burns, Mrs. Cullom, Mrs. Anderson, Mrs. Brown, Mrs. William Shaffer, and Mrs. Cromwell; (fourth row) Joy Spencer McClamroch, Mrs. William Morris, Mrs. Palmer, Belle Temple, Mrs. Hazelton, Cora Bracken Morris, and Mrs. Charles Gunther.

Boarding a train in Frankfort on December 2, 1940, are 4-H members, from left to right, Roberta Warren, Carroll Johnson, Esta Avery, and William Congleton, winners of the first Chicago trip merit award, sponsored by Clinton County Bank and Trust. They and their chaperone spent the day touring Chicago. That evening, they visited the Bismarck Hotel's ballroom, where they danced to big band music. (Carroll Johnson.)

Allen Wyrick (far left) shows his Angus steer to Paul Cullom (center left) and an unidentified man at the 1954 Clinton County Fair. Wyrick graduated Scircleville High School that same year and then attended Purdue University, graduating in 1958 with a degree in agriculture economy. He farmed in Johnson Township and was voted Indiana State Star Young Farmer in 1973. Today, Clinton County offers a memorial scholarship in his name. (Clinton County Extension Office.)

Thrasher's Department Store owner Milton B. Thrasher influenced much of Frankfort's development, including the interurban, for which he procured local rights-of-way. This 1929 photograph shows Thrasher diving into the Frankfort swimming pool at 77. A lifelong swimmer, Thrasher was featured in a 1934 *Ripley's Believe It or Not!* comic for his headfirst plunge into the pool from a 15-foot-high diving board at age 82. Thrasher died in 1937. (Greg Miller.)

The Frankfort Community Public Library's longest-serving head librarian was Edith Thompson, who joined the staff in 1924. After 44 years, she retired in September 1968, one month before her death. Thompson is remembered fondly as the consummate librarian—stately, efficient, soft-spoken, and loved by patrons. She is shown here in the mid-1950s vacationing in Hawaii. (Barbara Fausett.)

The members of the Tri Kappa Follies chorus pose in 1952, when they performed for a fundraiser for polio, which was prevalent throughout the county. The chorus's act that year ended with a moving rendition of "You'll Never Walk Alone." They are, from left to right, (first row) unidentified, Dorothy Noe, Helen Carroll, and Roberta Boggs; (second row) Lib Pickering, Ann Messick, Mary Ann Rogers, unidentified, and Toni Gill. (Jill Carroll.)

Members of the Frankfort Roller Aires Skating Club placed high in the 1976 national skating club competition in Toledo, Ohio. Pictured are, from left to right, Kim Wilson Ray, Missy Adams Hedges, Joni Seibert Percy, Tammy Adams Gregg, Jason Coleman, Jerri Howe, and K.C. Seibert. Home base for the skaters was the Hoosierland Roller Rink, built in 1949 north of TPA Park, where it still serves Frankfort-area skaters today. (Kim Ray.)

62

Five

HOMEGROWN HEROES

All five of Cleo and Gertrude Catron's sons volunteered for military service during World War II, but only four came home. Dee (top right) entered the Army in May 1941, Dale (center) volunteered in October 1942, and Glay (lower right) signed up the following February. Gayle (lower left) joined the Navy in May 1944, and Les (top left) joined in June, the same year Dale was reported missing in action. (John Catron.)

Civil War veteran John Sheets enlisted in the Union Army in 1862. He served three years and fought in numerous decisive battles, including Chickamauga, the siege of Chattanooga, and the Atlanta campaign throughout the summer of 1864. He rode with Wilson's Raid through Alabama and Georgia late in the war. A farmer, he lived eight miles north of Frankfort with his wife, Louvina, until 1931, when he died at 87.

Spanish-American War veteran Frank W. Barnett served as Clinton County treasurer from 1906 to 1908. He then became a construction contractor, helping to build several Indiana roads and highways. A native of Kirklin, he was born in 1868. He and wife, Zona, raised three daughters and two sons. He died in 1939 at the age of 71.

Company I, 28th Regiment was composed of Clinton County volunteers. Anticipating the declaration of war with Spain, they were already organized when their orders arrived Monday night, April 25, 1898. They boarded a train early the next morning and were first to report to Camp Mount on the Indiana State Fairgrounds. Later, the Clinton County men were mustered into service as Company C, 158th Indiana Volunteer Infantry. (Leroy Good.)

After the Spanish-American War ended, turmoil remained in the Philippines. So on September 11, 1899, 200 men from Clinton and adjoining counties traveled to St. Louis to enlist for Philippine service. They became Company I, 38th US Volunteers, and arrived in Manila on December 26. They were actively engaged there until they returned to the United States in May 1901. (Leroy Good.)

Frankfort honored fallen Spanish-American War hero Edward T. Bennett on April 7, 1899, with a funeral procession from the Columbia Theater to the IOOF Cemetery. A member of Company B, 16th Infantry, 22-year-old Bennett fought alongside the Rough Riders against Santiago, charging up San Juan Hill. He took ill and died in August 1896 in Cuba, where he was buried. Months later, the Army exhumed his body and shipped it home.

Roy Ramey, left, poses with three unidentified Army buddies at Camp Shelby, Hattiesburg, Mississippi, where, in 1917, they underwent training in preparation for World War I military service overseas. After the war, Roy and his brother Ray started Ramey Bros. Burial Vault Company in Frankfort. (Donna and William Huffer.)

Early on August 2, 1945, US Navy pilot Lt. Adrian Marks of Frankfort was dispatched to an area in the Western Pacific midway between the Philippines and Guam, where some 300 men had been spotted thrashing about in the water. They were the survivors of the USS *Indianapolis's* 1,200-man crew. The Navy was unaware that the ship had been torpedoed and sunk by the Japanese four days before. As Marks cruised over the men at a low altitude in his seaplane, he saw the sharks. Disregarding orders, Marks made a daring landing on the ocean in his seaplane. He and his crew started pulling men onboard and radioed for help. When the plane's fuselage was full, they carried men onto the wings and tied them in place with parachute cord. Marks and his gallant crew worked all night long. They saved 56 men. After the war, Marks joined his wife, Elta, in Frankfort, where he opened a law practice, specializing in real estate titles and deeds. Here, he displays an award of appreciation given him by the Air Force Association in 1990. He died March 7, 1998. (Wesley Manor.)

Twins Eldon, left, and Elvin Baker of Frankfort joined the Army at the start of World War II, enlisting shortly after the attack on Pearl Harbor. While fighting in Europe, Elvin was captured by Germans and held as prisoner for the duration of the war. Both brothers were honorably discharged from the Army in 1945. (Donna Mosson.)

Howard "Buzz" Hoehn takes a break from his World War II duties during a furlough on the island of Barbados. Hoehn joined the Army Air Corps in December 1942 and was trained as an airplane mechanic. He was discharged in November 1945, after serving almost a year on Guam. Hoehn and his wife, Doris, operated Hoehn Insurance in Frankfort for 40 years. (Buzz Hoehn.)

Paul Martin of Frankfort joined the Marines in 1943, serving in the South Pacific. Later, he and his wife, Margaret, raised two daughters, Julia and Janet. He helped set up and maintain the Little League baseball diamond at TPA Park and worked 40 years as a switchman for the Nickel Plate Railroad. He died in 2002. (Margaret "Pat" Rooker.)

Harold Stewart, right, of Frankfort poses for this 1943 photograph with two of his buddies while they were in Marine training at Camp Lejeune, North Carolina. During World War II, Stewart fought in the Battle of Okinawa. After the war, he returned to Frankfort, where he lived the rest of his life with his wife, Geneva. He passed away in February 2005. (Geneva Stewart.)

The 1938 Headquarters Company, 2nd Battalion, Frankfort, 151st Infantry of the Indiana National Guard is shown above. Members are, from left to right, (first row) L.O. Sanders, W.I. Sheets, C.E. Cue, J.F. Moudy, F.B. Mohler, and R.A. Taylor; (second row) L.A. Johnson, J.B. Meeks, R.G. Thornton, C.F. Boxwell, K.G. (Keith) Huffer, and L.C. Brown; (third row) T.O. Biddle, D.W. Payne, D.M. MacKenzie, J.P. Young, M.R. Lamm, C.R. Howe, and G.F. Skinner. (Donna and William Huffer.)

Hulbert D. Baker wears his Western Union uniform in this 1928 picture, but years later, he wore an Army uniform fighting in Normandy, France, during the D-Day invasion. For his heroism on June 8, 1944, he received the Bronze Star. The citation reads, "Private Baker courageously moved to an exposed position and by deliberately diverting hostile fire to himself, enabled his comrades to complete the important mission in comparative safety." (Donna Mosson.)

Headquarters Company, 2nd Battalion, 151st Regiment, 38th Infantry Division of the Indiana National Guard pose for this photograph in 1953 at Camp Grayling, Michigan. All of the guardsmen are from Clinton County. Identified are (first row) fourth from left, 1st Lt. Dennis Cantwell; and 12th from left, Master Sgt. Willard Wilson. (Willard and Marilyn Wilson.)

Earl Cripe entered the Army in February 1966, serving 12 months in Vietnam—three as a power train mechanic and nine as a door gunner and mechanic. During that time, he was shot down twice and walked away. He earned several medals and ribbons and was honorably discharged in February 1968. Retired from a career in heating and air-conditioning, he opened Travelers Pizzeria in Kirklin in 2013. (Earl Cripe.)

Clinton County dedicated its veterans' memorial on the south side of the courthouse on September 15, 2007. The project, led by Veterans Affairs officer Joe Root, honors county veterans who fought in every war since the Civil War. Speakers are, from left to right, Jim Buck, Nathan McCullough, Justin Hunter, Mayor Don Stock, US Representative Steve Buyer, Bill Beard, Mike Conner, Bernie Newhart, Eric Cupp, and Millard See. (Joe Root.)

Four US Air Force generals who originally called Frankfort home are memorialized with a monument on the Clinton County Courthouse lawn. The generals are: Lt. Gen. James F. Record, Lt. Gen. Jay W. Kelley, Brig. Gen. James W. Lucas, and Brig. Gen. James P. Ulm. Collectively, they earned over 35 major awards, commanded troops during combat, served all over the world, and made Clinton County proud. (Joe Root.)

Six

PLANES, TRAINS, AND AUTOMOBILES

In 1928, George Lockwood, left, built the Aero Inn on property adjoining the airstrip on State Road 39, two miles south of Frankfort. Tot Douglas managed the field, but Lockwood took it over in 1939 and named it Lockwood Field. After World War II, the Veterans Administration sponsored a civilian flight-training program there, which Lockwood's son Joe, right, managed. The Lockwoods are shown here in 1946. (Donna and William Huffer.)

A crowd gathered on June 22, 1930, at Clinton County's Lockwood Field to greet nationally known pilot Reg Robbins, who set a flight record the year before when he and mechanic James Kelly flew 172 hours, refueling in-flight 17 times. Robbins flew this special Ford trimotor airplane on a goodwill tour for the *Fort Worth Press*. (Leroy Good.)

FRANKFORT MUNICIPAL AIRPORT

GRAND OPENING · · · · · · · · ·

AIR SHOW

The Pioneers—1916

Development Era—1940

Fast, Proven Transportation—1972

Souvenir Program
June 11, 1972

25¢

Frankfort Municipal Airport opened in 1960 with one runway, a taxi strip, a fueling station, an administration building, and a small hangar. The city celebrated the airport's expansion 12 years later with a grand opening and air show, attracting approximately 5,000 attendees. The day started with a fly-in breakfast and continued until dark with skydiving, fly-bys, gliders, antique planes, Snoopy, and the Red Baron. (Donna and William Huffer.)

The first railroad track was laid in Clinton County in 1852, and within 50 years, Frankfort was a railroad hub. By 1873, railroad expansion was exploding with companies starting, expanding, and merging to form new intrastate and interstate routes. Among the original lines serving Frankfort were the Frankfort-Kokomo Railroad, the Vandalia Company, the Monon, and the Clover Leaf, which later became the Nickel Plate, a Frankfort mainstay for many years, and now the Norfolk-Southern. Above, a Lake Erie & Western steam locomotive chugs through town in 1900. By then, railroads were essential to the local commerce, providing jobs for one out of every three working men, while transporting the products of local industries and farms to market and hauling in their supplies. Below, new Nickel Plate diesel locomotives move into the roundhouse around 1950. (Both, Leroy Good.)

This Frankfort railroad crew gathers on a 1950s winter day. They are, from left to right, (first row) Floyd Lowder, Harley Beard, Leonard Hall, Wilburn Coy, Bill Rich, Raymond Kressell, Hugh Cockrum, Fred Birge, Fern McCory, and Matthew Barber; (second row) Lawrence Pedigo, Leroy Malicoat, Fletcher Reed, Art Rickert, Ted Rich, Ted Hodson, Bill Cockrum, Basil Reed, Ben Taylor, Arthur Price, Bob Fink, Mervin Fisher, Bill Chamber, and Frank Jacobs.

Longtime Nickel Plate employee Grover Huffer leans out the window of the dining car while it is parked in the Frankfort yards around 1950. Huffer was a cook, preparing meals for the railroad maintenance crews for several years. Approaching the car is Huffer's nephew Bill. (Donna and William Huffer.)

Members of the Boilermakers Local No. 364 pose around 1940. Identified are (first row) second from left, Francis "Pig" Lipp; fourth from left, Jack Lipp; (third row) first from left, Willie T. Curtis. Boilermakers worked at the roundhouse, maintaining the old steam locomotives. They also fired up the coals in the locomotive's boilers and kept them running. Boilermakers, like the steam locomotives, were largely obsolete by the mid-1960s. (Steve Greeno.)

Train wrecks occurred frequently throughout the early 20th century with often tragic outcomes. The wreck pictured is believed to be the crash of the No. 41 Clover Leaf freight train on June 12, 1912, east of Frankfort city limits. A broken flange on one of the gondolas was deemed the probable cause. Three men died when they were crushed by a load of heavy pipes. (Leroy Good.)

Edmund Peele, an employee of the Frankfort, Kokomo & Western Traction Company, poses with his daughter Lettie Mae in the yard of their Frankfort home about 1914. The FK&WT formed in 1911 and opened a 26-mile line between Frankfort and Kokomo in July 1912. Shortly after, it merged into the Indiana Railways & Light Company. The depot occupied the southeast corner of North Main and West Morrison Streets. (Greg Townsend.)

Below, the Alliance Construction Company's work gang grades the road under the newly built viaduct on Freeman Street in December 1916. This bridge and another over Armstrong Street were part of the roadway for the Indianapolis & Frankfort Railroad. Both viaducts are in use today. (Neil Conner.)

The parade was the high point of the Indiana Grand Army of the Republic (GAR) Encampment, which Frankfort hosted June 3–5, 1924. Hailed as its "crowning feature," the parade drew thousands of cheering spectators. One of the parade's highlights is this trackless locomotive, which advertised the LykGlas Auto Renual painting system. Harry J. Burkhalter, whose name appears at the bottom of the banner, was a Frankfort mechanic. (Leroy Good.)

Frankfort coal and oil dealer Fred H. Paul and his son Sam built their "roadable" locomotive with a 1949 school bus chassis and a 60-year-old steam engine Fred found in an old chicken house. Sam drew the boiler plans, which garnered the Society of Mechanical Engineers' required approval. The locomotive, finished in 1959, took two years to build. Sam still refers to the locomotive as "Dad's toy." (Sam Paul.)

The Clinton County Auto Show, January 11–13, 1917, attracted hundreds of car enthusiasts and featured scores of new models, including the short-lived Highlander to be assembled in Frankfort. Local dealers Frank Blinn, Dick Bush, Philip Dorner, and George Thurman were among the exhibitors. The event occupied the Tabernacle, a temporary structure built on the site of the future Howard Hall, and was dismantled shortly after this event. (William Goodwin Miller.)

Frankfort's first Ford dealer, George B. Thurman, poses with a Model T around 1912. He later sold and serviced Whippet-Durrant vehicles on East Washington Street. For a brief time, he operated Thurman Jewelry store in downtown Frankfort with his son. He also served as a city councilman and became known as "the father of TPA Park" because of his efforts in its establishment. He died in 1949 at age 85.

Goodwin Funeral Home's 1934 Packard ambulance/hearse is parked in front of the Goodwin home at 200 South Main Street. William Goodwin can be seen standing on the porch with his mother, Lillian, to his left, and his wife, Katherine, to his right. (William Goodwin Miller.)

William Goodwin and his mother, Lillian Epperson Goodwin, stand next to a relic of their family's past—a horse-drawn cab. The photograph was taken in 1957 at Goodwin Funeral Home. Goodwin inherited the family business from his father, John Charles, in 1926. When Goodwin died in 1996 at age 93, he was the oldest active funeral director in Indiana. (William Goodwin Miller.)

Thousands attended a pushmobile race held October 21, 1932, in conjunction with the county's annual corn show. Guests included the secretary of the American Pushmobile Association and a racecar builder from the Indianapolis Speedway. Colver Machine & Iron Works' car No. 4, driven by Jack Miller, won the main event—20 laps around the courthouse square. The prize was $10. The pushers were called the race's "unsung heroes."

US Hame Manufacturing Company (USHCO) assembled more than 12,000 bodies for Plymouth's line of woodies—station wagons characterized by wooden side panels—between 1937 and 1950 at its Frankfort factory at 555 Hoke Avenue. Completed bodies were shipped to Detroit for finishing. USHCO's origins trace back to the mid-1800s, when it made hames—supports for horse collars. The Frankfort plant was in business until 1950, when Chrysler discontinued woodies. (William Goodwin Miller.)

Seven

MAIN STREET
AND BEYOND

Cutbacks in the railroad's workforce might have thrust Frankfort's economy into a tailspin in the early 1950s if not for a group of forward-thinking local businessmen who established the industrial park west of town. Its ideal location, with access to State Road 28 and rail service, first attracted Peter Paul Cadbury in 1955. Other factories, such as National Seal, shown here, soon followed, providing hundreds of jobs and contributing to the local economy.

GEO. Y FOWLER

"He was a scholar, and a ripe and good one , exceeding wise, fair spoken."
—*Henry VIII*

This caricature, drawn around 1900, depicts George Y. Fowler, the *Times'* founder/publisher. Born in 1860, Fowler entered the business at age 14 as an apprentice at the *Frankfort Crescent* and, after 11 years, struck out on his own, starting the *Weekly Times*. He converted it to a daily publication, the *Frankfort Morning Times*, in April 1894. An innovative businessman, Fowler replaced handset type with a Linotype and purchased the newest and fastest presses available. When he died at age 54 in 1914, his sons Raymond, Walter, and Max, who then was 20, took over. Max ran the *Times* until he died in 1960, and the business was passed on to his heirs. They sold it to Nixon Newspapers Inc. in May 1969.

Frankfort-born Basil "Stuffy" Walters started his newspaper career as telegraph editor for the *Indianapolis Star* in 1920. After a year, he moved on to other city papers, earning promotions to assistant editor, editor, executive editor, and finally vice president of the *Chicago Daily News*. Walters retired to Frankfort in 1961 and was inducted into Indiana's Journalism Hall of Fame in 1973. He died in 1975. (Indiana Journalism Hall of Fame.)

Ray Moscowitz joined the *Frankfort Morning Times* in 1964 as a reporter. After a stint in Dayton, Ohio, from 1965 to 1969, he returned to Frankfort as managing editor. He later headed other city papers within the *Times'* parent company chain, Nixon Newspapers Inc., finally retiring as editorial director. Moscowitz, one of seven Journalism Hall of Fame inductees with Frankfort ties, was inducted in 2002 and served as president from 2008 to 2013. (Ray Moscowitz.)

Frankfort's premier broadcaster Vern Kaspar (above and below, left) got his start in Sioux City, Iowa, in 1936 at age 13, when he obtained his FCC license in amateur radio. After several years of broadcasting experience, Kaspar moved his family to Frankfort in 1959, purchasing WILO and forming Kaspar Broadcasting. Later, Kasper traveled extensively as a member of the National Broadcast Editorial Association. One of those trips took him to Beirut, Lebanon, where he and a small group of journalists met and interviewed Yasser Arafat, below, then head of the Palestine Liberation Organization. Locally, WILO listeners have tuned in Kaspar weekday mornings for many years as he interviews guests, takes calls, and expresses his strong views. Kaspar was inducted into the Indiana Broadcast Hall of Fame in 2004. Today, he runs the Frankfort station with his son Russ. (Both, Russ Kaspar.)

Aughe's Sewing Machine and Gun Shop was located on the north side of the square at the corner of Washington and Jackson Streets from 1884 until 1902, when it was torn down to make way for a new bank. Frank Aughe and his son, Karl, ran the business and repaired all types of guns and small machines.

Occupying the former Aughe business site, Frankfort's American National Bank opened in 1902 with $100,000 in reserve, according to Volume No. 64 of *The Bankers Magazine*. John A. Ross was the bank's first president, and Robert Bracken was the cashier. Frankfort's American National Bank closed around 1930, but the building is still standing.

This photograph was taken at the C.M. Stewart general store, located at 1252 West Morrison Street, in 1920 when the store opened. Owner Clarence M. Stewart is seated behind the counter. The young man standing nearby could not be identified but is likely the store employee who delivered customers' purchases by bicycle. (Geneva Stewart.)

German-born Philip Dorner immigrated to America in 1852 at age 25, ultimately settling in Frankfort. A tanner by trade, he established his own tannery on East Washington Street in 1867. He later expanded the business, selling harnesses and leather goods. He also manufactured buggies and eventually assumed a Chevrolet franchise, which his family maintained until the 1970s. Dorner and his wife, Mary, raised nine children. He died in 1905.

Campbell's Coffee Shop was located at 210 North Main Street near Washington Street in the late 1920s. Pictured are Mabel Irene and Frank Campbell standing at the counter. Their son, Eddie, is behind them. The Campbells later owned and operated a grocery store on Rossville Avenue. (Richard Lee Campbell.)

William Comly, left, and his brother-in-law Clem Thompson stand outside the Wm. M. Comly, Funeral Director storefront at 56 South Main Street around 1895. Comly offered a full line of funeral reservoirs, vases, steel wire settees, and chairs for lawns and cemeteries. He was Frankfort's first city clerk, elected in 1875, and later served as fire chief for eight years. Thompson owned the piano and organ store.

An audience, eager for the evening's feature film to roll, packs the Palace Picture Parlor. The Palace was located at 52 South Main Street and operated only from 1914 through 1916, when it closed unexpectedly. The Roxy later occupied the location.

M.L. Conley built the Conley Theater in 1922 at the corner of Walnut and Jackson Streets from the gutted remains of the Blinn Theater, which burned in 1920. Shown here, pasted to the side of the theater, is a poster advertising the 1935 film *Oh, Daddy*, starting November 29. Less than two months later, M.L. Conley sold his theater to the Roxy owners, who also ran the Princess Theater.

Kids flocked to the Roxy Theater Saturday mornings during the 1950s with bottle caps to exchange for admission to a movie picked just for them. The Roxy was a Frankfort landmark at 52–56 South Main Street until it was demolished in 1974 and became the parking lot for Citizens Building and Loan Association. The Roxy opened November 4, 1931. The last film was shown there on June 19, 1973. (Barbara Fausett.)

The Roxy Theater's usherettes and snack bar attendants gather for this early 1940s photograph. Back in Hollywood's golden era, movie theaters staffed polished, professional usherettes, whose purpose was to ensure that their movie-going audience's experience was a pleasant one. Those identified are (first row) center, Bonnie Lou Clark; (second row) right, Delores Corbett; (third row) fifth from left, Phyllis Kellogg Johnson. (Steve Greeno.)

Tailor John B. Meifeld operated a shop and later a real estate investment business on the square for 53 years. Here, he and his employees pose for this 1895 photograph. From left to right are Albert Van Camp, Meifeld, Mabel Steele, Mary Heinbaugh, Laura Thomas, Charley Mickley, and Henry Heiden. Meifeld's business philosophy is perhaps demonstrated in the sign on the wall that reads, "Strangers Will Please Make Deposit on All Orders."

In 1942, Woolworth employees pose for this photograph when the store was located on the southwest corner of Clinton and Jackson Streets. Those identified are Virginia Mundell (second from left), Delores Kaylor (second from front, second row), and Doris Kelly (third from right). Woolworth's opened in Frankfort in 1912. It later moved to the northwest corner of Clinton and Main Streets until it closed in 1986. (Steve Greeno.)

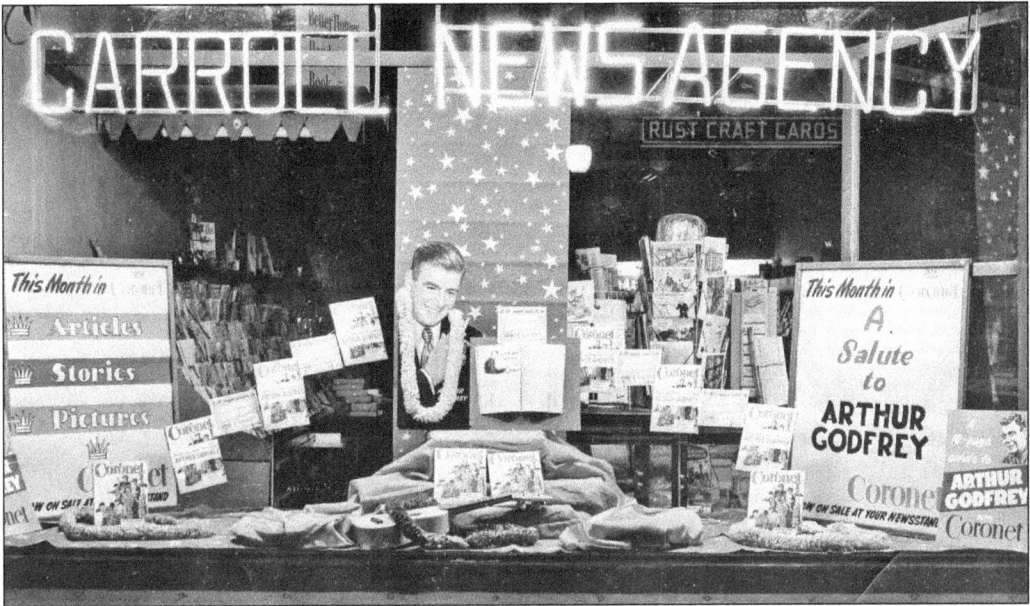

The Carroll News Agency's window often displayed magazine promotions, such as this for the June 1953 edition of *Coronet*. Arthur and Helen Carroll opened the shop at 258 North Main Street in 1945. They renamed it Carroll's Card Shop in the mid-1950s. Known as the place to buy hard-to-find items, it stocked greeting cards, party supplies, invitations, newspapers, and magazines. Carroll's closed in 1989, three years after Arthur's death. (Jill Carroll.)

Diana Shop manager Helen Young Edington, right, chats with coworker Dorothy Widner about ladies' hats in 1969. The store, located on the south side of the square at 63 East Clinton Street, was a popular ladies' clothing shop that served the community during the 1960s and 1970s. (Sue Rodkey.)

Members, friends, and family of the Ingram-Richardson Athletic Association gather for their annual picnic in TPA Park on a sunny, late summer Saturday in 1924. Ingram-Richardson Company, manufacturer of enamel tabletops, opened its Frankfort operation in 1917. The new factory provided relief for its busy Beaver Falls, Pennsylvania, factory and fulfilled orders from the Midwest. Over the 65 years that Ing-Rich operated in Frankfort, it provided employment for

Ingram-Richardson Company officials break ground for the new factory in 1916. Pictured are, from left to right, unidentified, Ernest Richardson, Wallace G. Himmelwright, Clyde Masters, three unidentified, Charles P. McDougall, and Louis Ingram.

94

thousands of area workers. When the plant closed in January 1981, its president blamed a sagging housing market, high energy costs, and excessive government regulations. The workers, however, rejected that rationale, asserting that management had forced them to perform inefficiently in an effort to curb costs. (Donna and William Huffer.)

Peoples Life Insurance Company was founded in 1906. By 1916, it had grown into a new, six-story office building constructed of concrete and steel, located on the northeast corner of Main and Walnut Streets. The building is shown here decorated for the GAR Encampment hosted by Frankfort in 1924. The building was torn down in the summer of 1969. Today, the site is a parking lot for Farmers Bank.

Ernest Black, center, was a longtime agent for Peoples Life Insurance Company. This photograph, taken in May 1914, shows Black with two unidentified associates. Unfortunately, he died in 1922 at age 39, leaving a widow and three young children. According to his obituary, he was respected for his "keen foresight and excellent judgment." (Marilyn Wilson.)

The Coulter Hotel opened in 1876 on the southeast corner of Jackson and Clinton Streets and was the hotel of choice for Frankfort's visiting dignitaries. The Coulter offered amenities found at big-city, luxury hotels—elegant dining room, barbershop, shoeshine stand, porters, maids, and transportation to and from the depots. However, by 1964, the hotel faced terminal financial ills. It closed in 1966; a wrecking ball took it down in 1967.

Clinton County Hospital was built in its present location on South Jackson Street in 1923, replacing a medical facility that had occupied the second floor of Kern Furniture Store since 1899. A west wing was added in 1953, and after the county council appropriated $5 million in 1978, citizens pledged $2 million more, funding another wing built early in 1980. The original structure was demolished shortly after. (Carroll Johnson.)

Standing on the steam traction engine is Fred H. Paul around 1900. The machines belonged to Paul's father, who owned and operated the Hillisburg-based Paul Coal Company, the first coal company between Frankfort and Tipton. The senior Paul also had the largest independent threshing ring east of the Mississippi River with 12 steam threshers. (Sam Paul.)

Thomas O. Wade and his son, Thurl O. "Pete" Wade, drilled water wells throughout the Clinton County area during the late 1800s and several years into the 1900s. Pete drilled many wells in the western part of the city to serve the railroad. Thomas is shown standing nearest the rig around 1900. (Margaret "Pat" Rooker.)

An unidentified employee of National Handle Company checks his load of logs. The factory, located on West Barner Street, started in 1888. At its peak, the company produced an average of 150 hoe and fork handles a day and supported a workforce of 125. (Greg Miller.)

Milk and cream did not always come from the grocery store. When this photograph was taken around 1925, the unidentified Schlosser Brothers Creamery milkman was delivering dairy products to his customer. The creamery was located at Columbia and Morrison Streets. The Delphi Wagon Works built the truck.

Associates of Black Agency Real Estate, 607 West Walnut Street, line up for this picture in the mid-1970s. From left to right, they are Ruth Voorhees, Gloria Crum, Everett Emery, owner John Black, Ivan Spencer, secretary-broker Jan Archibald (Black's granddaughter), Joe Summers, Marge Johnson, Virginia Hackerd, Phyllis Bates, and Bob Wyrick. (Marilyn Wilson.)

Within a week of the new Orlando-based Walt Disney World 1971 opening, Frankfort's Indiana Brass was preparing to ship out 3,248 lavatory, bath, and shower fittings destined for Disney World's use at the Court of Flags. In this October 5, 1971, photograph, Indiana Brass employee Ruby Emory gives the faucets a final inspection.

Eight

COMMUNITY HUBS

Frankfort's original library was a small collection of books that moved from location to location before settling into a room at the high school in 1900. In 1905, a $24,000 gift from Andrew Carnegie funded a library building on West Clinton Street, shown here in the 1950s. Since then, the Frankfort Community Public Library has grown into a cultural center that includes a theater, art galleries, and many other amenities.

Frankfort, Ind.

Pilgrim Holiness College and Theological Seminary opened on Frankfort's southwest side in 1927. Closing temporarily during the Depression, it reopened in 1939 as Frankfort Pilgrim College, serving the Pilgrim Holiness Church until 1968. At that time, Pilgrim Holiness merged with the Wesleyan Methodist Church, and the college was renamed Frankfort Wesleyan Bible College. It closed in 1972 when it merged with a Wesleyan college in Pennsylvania. (Connie Carlson.)

Frankfort's First Presbyterian Church was established in a log cabin in 1831 by a congregation of 17. Their first building was erected at its present West Clinton Street location in 1833 and was replaced with a modest brick structure in 1857. The current church was built in 1876 with two giant steeples, which were removed during the Depression due to maintenance costs. The congregation has about 300 members today. (Carroll Johnson.)

The First Christian Church congregation gathers March 27, 1893, for the dedication of its new sanctuary on the northwest corner of Columbia and Walnut Streets, shown above. A guest pastor from Cincinnati, who informed parishioners that the building committee was short $7,500 in meeting expenses, led the meeting. He then announced that he intended to raise that amount that very day, and he did. The congregation originally met in a wooden building on this site in 1830. Later, it moved to a building on Jackson Street but returned to Columbia and Walnut Streets in 1892 to build the present church. Below, the congregation's men join forces on May 8, 1912, to build a tabernacle, in which Sunday school classes and revivals would be held. The building was completed in a day. (Both, First Christian Church.)

First Baptist Church's 1963 children's choir, under the direction of Pat Harwood (second row, far right) poses on the church's front steps. Below is the church as it appeared in the 1950s, very much as it appears today. The local Baptists held meetings as early as 1830 in locations around the county. In 1860, they made their first attempt at organizing a First Baptist Church, meeting for a while in the courthouse, but the effort waned. Five Baptists tried again in 1879 and succeeded, meeting above a store on the town square until they dedicated their first church building in 1882. That building was destroyed by a tornado in 1913, but the 198 members immediately rebuilt. In 1959, the First Baptist Church added an education wing. Today, it has 325 members. (Left, Kim Ray.)

The congregation of Frankfort's First Methodist Episcopal Church, 257 South Main Street, gathers in its sanctuary on October 2, 1932, for its centennial pageant. The church dropped "Episcopal" from its name in 1939 and became known as First Methodist Church. It moved to its current location on Wilshire Drive in 1966 and, two years later, changed its name to St. Matthew United Methodist Church. (St. Matthew UMC.)

The participants in First Methodist Episcopal Church's vacation Bible school pose for their class picture on June 28, 1931, at the church. Standing in the back row, center, with the teachers is the church's Pastor Claude McClure. (St. Matthew UMC.)

Thousands of country music lovers flocked to Shady Acres Ranch, one of Indiana's most popular outdoor entertainment venues, from the late 1940s through the late 1950s. Situated on State Road 38 in northwestern Clinton County, Shady Acres was carved out of 18 wooded acres belonging to Owen Skiles. Partner Curley Myers financed the operation, handled promotion, and booked the talent. Some of the brightest country music stars of that time—Roy Acuff, Rex Allen, Gene Autry, Little Jimmy Dickens, and Pee Wee King among them—thrilled Shady Acres audiences. Local talent—Bob Coapstick, Keith Kallner, Bob Harshman, Glen Davis, Jimmy Gross, Evelyn Perry, and Myers—formed the house band, the Shady Acres Ranch Gang. Shows were family-oriented, starting after church on Sundays. Shady Acres flourished until 1957, when television programming began to keep people home. The ranch closed shortly after.

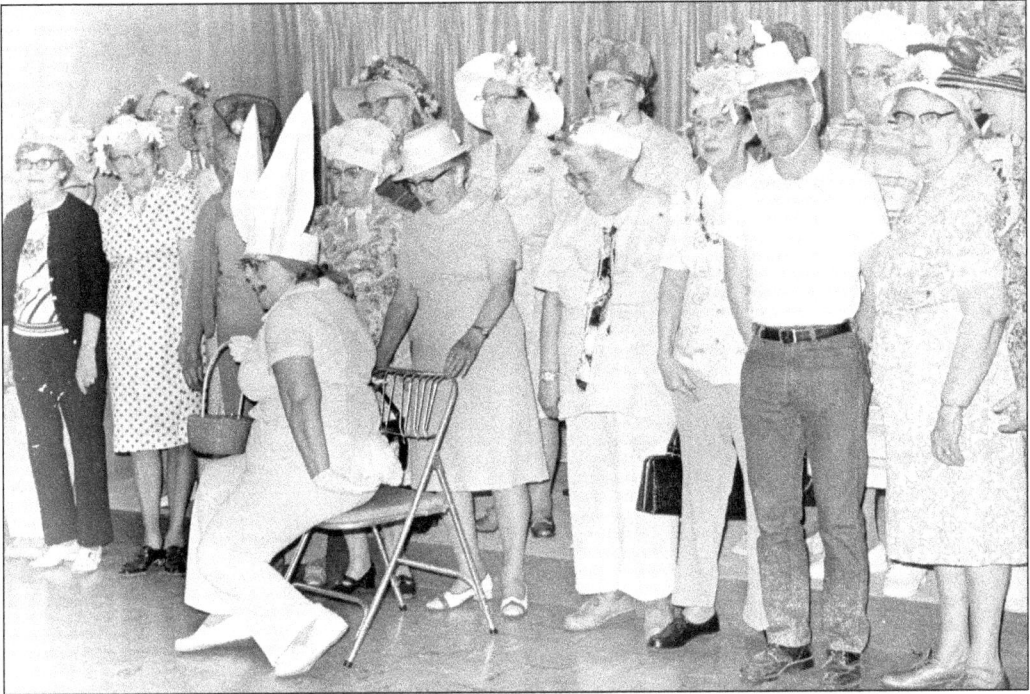

Above, Aileen Ford, seated, and van driver Dan McCly, second from right, join the judges on April 15, 1976, for the annual Easter bonnet contest at the Paul Phillippe Resource Center. Below, Elmer Rex, the gentleman on the left, and Joe Noble give Faye Ayers a kiss on November 28, 1978, surrounded by, from left to right, Orpha Faust, Nellie Weida, and Elsie Stewart. The center was established in 1965 in the former St. Mary's Catholic School building at Walnut and Second Streets as the Human Resource Center to provide services to Clinton County seniors. It was renamed the Paul Phillippe Resource Center in 1974 to honor the memory of one of the center's most devoted members, and in the intervening years, it has expanded its space and services. (Both, Paul Phillippe Resource Center.)

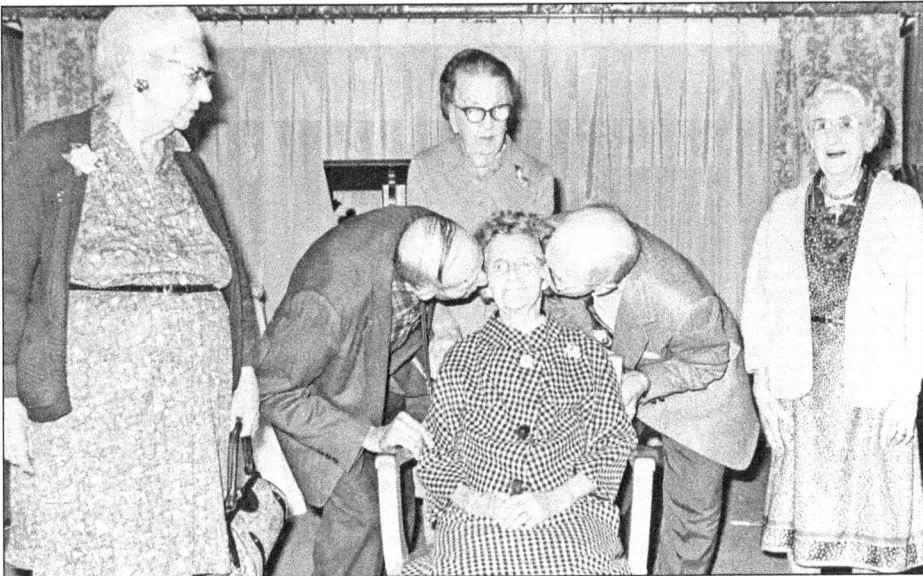

The Red Barn Theater is a professional, non-equity company located a mile east of Frankfort. Founded in 1968 by Frankfort High School drama teacher Martin Henderson and his wife, Carol Ann, it has operated as a nonprofit endeavor every year since. The Hendersons converted a decades-old barn into a modern venue that seats 200. Each season, they stage four productions—three plays and a musical. (Carol Ann and Martin Henderson.)

From left to right, Mayor Roy Scott, then-director of the Paul Phillippe Resource Center Jo Ellen Ogle, and Ayten Rogowski of WILO chat with Gov. Frank O'Bannon on July 31, 2003, at Frankfort's Neighborhood Center. O'Bannon was there to promote his economic plans for the state while showing his support for Scott's re-election. Sadly, O'Bannon died six weeks later after suffering a stroke. (Paul Phillippe Resource Center.)

Nine

MONUMENTAL MOMENTS

In the predawn hours of November 14, 1975, the *Times'* Clinton Street building was destroyed after a former employee started a fire to conceal an attempted burglary. Employees moved into temporary offices the next day and resumed production. They moved into a new, permanent building two years later. Ivy Tech took over the building in 2013 for its new Frankfort campus. (Mary Patchett/ Frankfort Community Public Library.)

The United States declared war on Germany on Friday, April 6, 1917. Two days later, 3,000 Frankfort residents braved the spring chill to dedicate Easter Sunday to the honor of Old Glory by raising a giant flag up a 100-foot pole erected by Clover Leaf Railroad employees. At 2:30 p.m., thousands—including citizens, policemen, firefighters, military veterans, GAR members, postal workers, railroad employees, and the Frankfort Boys Band—marched west on Clinton

Street, heading for the Clover Leaf shops. Waiting were speakers and patriotic music. Lafayette Pryor explained what the war would mean for Frankfort, the Rev. E.D. Salkeid offered a prayer, and Judge Combs spoke about labor's part in the war effort. The band accompanied the crowd as it sang "The Star Spangled Banner" while the flag was raised, and an honor guard fired three shots. (Donna and William Huffer.)

Thousands gather around the Clinton County Courthouse on November 14, 1918, shortly after receiving news that World War I had ended. The *Frankfort Morning Times* described the 20-hour festivities as the "wildest, happiest and biggest celebration of the city's young life." Joy-filled celebrants cheered the passing parade that featured numerous effigies of the defeated German kaiser. Flags; noisemakers of every description, including the saw-blade cymbals, shown below; and fireworks added to the historic revelry. The newspaper reported that "Grizzled veterans of the war that preserved the American union and healthy, youthful lads who were eagerly waiting their call to help civilization . . . men from all sorts of life—the high and the humble, the saint and the sinner—had a proud place in that colorful, kaleidoscopic, and tremendously impressive line." (Above, Leroy Good; below, Steve Greeno.)

Charles W. Fairbanks, left, was the guest of honor at Frankfort's Arbor Day celebration on April 16, 1914. Fairbanks, an Indiana senator (1897–1905) and vice president serving under Pres. Theodore Roosevelt (1905–1909), was president of the Indiana Forest Association. Shortly after Fairbanks's arrival, he joined Mayor Oliver Gard, Judge Joseph Combs (pictured on the right), J.C. Morrison, M. Epstein, and Fred Coulter for a motor tour of the city. Stops along the way included the city schools, where faculties and student bodies enthusiastically greeted the former vice president. At each school, Fairbanks spoke and helped students plant trees. At Third Ward, below, the students waved flags and cheered as the procession arrived. The *Frankfort Weekly Times* reported that a few minutes later, as the procession pulled away, the students sent it off with a "Chautauqua salute" (waving handkerchiefs).

The *Frankfort Weekly Crescent* estimated that 30,000 people had gathered on October 23, 1896, in downtown Frankfort to hear a speech by populist Democrat and US presidential candidate William Jennings Bryan during his first of three bids for the office. Prior to his arrival, the city, decorated in red, white, and blue, held a parade and hosted bands from several towns throughout the county. Keeping an ambitious schedule as he made his way through the Midwest, Bryan arrived in Frankfort by rail at 2:20 p.m., over an hour late. He was enormously popular, and the newspaper reported that when he stepped onto the podium, the crowd cheered for 10 minutes. He was presented with an elegant hickory cane made by "free silver Republicans" employed at Carter's handle factory in Frankfort. The *Crescent* predicted that Bryan would defeat his Republican opponent, William McKinley, on November 3. He did not, of course. But in Clinton County, when the votes were tallied, Bryan beat McKinley 3,747 to 3,607. (Leroy Good.)

Bryan made his second Frankfort stop October 17, 1912, arriving over the traction line. Several Frankfort officials, including Judge Joseph Combs and Congressman Martin A. Morrison, accompanied him. The crowd, roughly a tenth of that greeting him in 1896, was no less enthusiastic about Bryan's chances of winning the presidency against the Bull Moose Party's Theodore Roosevelt and Republican Woodrow Wilson. Bryan spoke for 30 minutes and then headed for Lafayette. (Leroy Good.)

Introducing Bryan was a 50-year-old Frankfort native, Congressman Martin Andrew Morrison. A former county attorney and school board member, he was elected to the US Congress in 1909, representing Indiana's ninth district for three terms. In 1925, he joined the legal staff of the Federal Trade Commission, from which he retired in 1942, maintaining his residence in Washington, DC. He died in Virginia in 1944. (Library of Congress.)

Thousands of spectators gathered around the platform of vice presidential candidate Richard Nixon's campaign train when it arrived in Frankfort at 12:40 p.m. October 16, 1952. "I Like Ike" buttons dotted lapels and caps, and "Welcome Pat and Dick Nixon" and "Dick Nixon—He's Our Boy" signs fanned the air. Accompanying the Nixons were Indiana GOP senators William Jenner and Homer Capehart, who spoke briefly from the train's rear platform. Afterward, Mayor and Mrs. Goder presented the Nixons with keys to the city—a mounted ring of brass keys inscribed "Dick and Pat Nixon, Frankfort, Indiana, 1952," fashioned as a door knocker by Frankfort's Indiana Brass. Nixon expressed his appreciation, followed by a 15-minute address. Immediately after, with the crowd still cheering, the train pulled out, headed for its next stop. (Above, Jill Carroll; below, Steve Greeno.)

Clinton County celebrated its centennial over four days—Saturday, September 6 through Tuesday, September 9, 1930. Activities kicked off Saturday on the courthouse lawn with the coronation of Centennial queen Fern Alexander, above. Sunday saw the dedication of the log cabin at TPA Park, a historical fashion show, a band concert, and a pageant depicting 100 years of progress for an audience of some 8,000 people. The Centennial Parade, below, was reportedly two miles long as it wound through Frankfort on Monday afternoon. It was followed by the dedication of the Daughters of the American Revolution marker at the courthouse, a display of historical relics, and a repeat of the pageant. Tuesday, the celebration's last day, featured a tennis tournament, a parade at the fairgrounds, and the American Legion's car giveaway. Thousands attended the centennial events, and the Centennial Committee called it a resounding success.

On April 29, 1910, fire destroyed the M.B. Thrasher Department Store and all its merchandise. Damage to the Coulter Opera House block, where Thrasher's was located, was over $90,000. Within six months of the fire, the store that had occupied the northeast corner of Jackson and Washington Streets since 1897 reopened. It remained in business in that location until 1988, when it permanently closed its doors. (Greg Miller.)

The memory of the devastating fire at Thrasher's prompted firefighters to react quickly on May 17, 1910, when fire broke out at Shortle Dry Goods store. The rapid response was credited with saving the building from total destruction. Bystanders were credited too for rushing inside the smoke-filled building to remove hundreds of bolts of silks and dress fabrics. Damage was estimated at $25,000. Shortle reopened February 28, 1911.

Fortunately, the fire that broke out in B.F. Cohee and Son Dry Goods store on April 29, 1914, was contained to the building's second floor. The steel ceiling and heavy floor prevented the flames from eating their way to the first floor, sparing most of the merchandise. The next day, Walter Cohee ran an ad in the newspaper thanking the firefighters and citizens for saving his store. (Leroy Good.)

Firefighters battle a massive blaze as it takes down an entire quarter block at the northwest corner of Washington and Main Streets on August 24, 1989. The fire destroyed five buildings containing six businesses. Among them was the Bon Merritt Drug Store. The city later rehabilitated the corner as a small park, bordered on two sides by a mural. (Jerry Leonard, Classic Frankfort.)

Knee deep and then some
5th St.
Photo By Shawow.

Arguably, the worst flood in Indiana history occurred Easter weekend 1913. No town with even a creek flowing through it escaped the catastrophic storm that started Friday, March 21, and poured until Tuesday. In Frankfort, one man died in front of Hertz Dry Goods when falling bricks struck him. Roofs were peeled off, windows broken, utility poles downed, and railroad tracks obstructed. The wind ripped off the grain elevator's roof and drove it into a house 360 feet away. Prairie Creek overflowed its banks, flooding the city's north, south, and southwest areas. By Tuesday, residents on the southwest side had sustained the heaviest damage. Many who remained in their homes were forced to seek refuge on their roofs awaiting rescue workers with boats. Countywide, floodwaters washed away six bridges, and roads were impassable. (Both, Greg Miller.)

The Lehman & Rosenthall flax mill occupied this site on Kyger Street, when at 6:55 a.m., March 11, 1880, the boiler exploded, killing eight men. The *Frankfort Daily Crescent* reported that the blast rocked the entire community and hurled bricks and shrapnel hundreds of feet in all directions. Numbers in the photograph correspond to where each fatality was found. The newspaper called it the city's worst tragedy. (Greg Miller.)

Smallpox swept the nation after the Spanish-American War, and Frankfort was not immune. On September 26, 1902, the city council passed a smallpox quarantine to be observed by infected residences, as well as hotels, where guests were found suffering with the illness. In October 1902, according to the Indiana State Board of Health, 35 counties reported 298 cases of smallpox; 12 of them, including two deaths, occurred in Clinton County.

SMALL POX

All persons are forbidden to enter or leave these premises without special permit from the Health Officer having jurisdiction, and all persons are forbidden to remove or mutilate this card or to in any way interfere with this quarantine without orders from said Health Offier.

PENALTY—A fine of **Ten to Fifty Dollars** to which may be added imprisonment.   By Order of

CLINTON COUNTY HEALTH COMMISSIONER

As freezing rain pounded Frankfort on January 10, 1930, broken tree limbs tore into homes and took down electrical wires, shown above. A 30-foot steel pole on the courthouse square toppled under the weight of the ice-laden wires. Sixty-one years later, ice devastated Frankfort again. Below, the great ice storm of March 12, 1991, brought the county to a standstill for a week. Streets, littered with broken limbs, were impassable, while heavy ice snapped utility poles in two, leaving them crisscrossed over county roads. Although power was out countywide, many businesses operated under generator power to provide crucial services. Mayor Don Snyder declared a civil emergency, and Gov. Evan Bayh declared the county a disaster. Damage was estimated at almost $4 million. Despite utility workers' herculean efforts, power was not fully restored for nearly three weeks. (Below, Mary Patchett/Frankfort Community Public Library.)

Above, two men assess the wreckage of Herb Heise's garage in Moran after a tornado swept through on June 20, 1942, pinning Heise beneath the rubble for 30 minutes. The tornado devastated northern Clinton County before entering Howard County, where it claimed four lives and injured hundreds. The storm's path was similar to that of the devastating April 11, 1965, Palm Sunday tornadoes that ripped through central Indiana, killing 137 people. No one in Clinton County was severely injured in that storm, although hundreds experienced the terrifying twisters. Below is what remained of the Owen Township School near Moran after the 1965 storm. Similar sights were plentiful throughout northern Clinton County. Barbara Taylor will never forget how the truck carrying her and her family outran the tornado that chased them. Many county residents share equally terrifying tales. (Above, Willard and Barbara Wilson; below, Barbara Taylor.)

When the Redpath Chautauqua train rolled into Frankfort, the festival pitched a giant tent and stayed a week. This photograph, taken around 1903, shows the event on West Washington Street (note the First Presbyterian Church steeples in the background). Chautauquas originated in 1868 and traveled the nation from 1903 to 1930, offering something for everyone—singers, musicians, poets, actors, lectures, politicians, and advocates for the latest movements sweeping the country.

The city threw a street party October 29, 1954, to celebrate throwing the switch on its new fluorescent streetlights. The $70,000 installation, designed by General Electric, was part of the city's effort to attract new industry. It contained 153 lights mounted on 30-foot poles around the courthouse square and along adjacent side streets. The city council boasted that Frankfort was the first city in Indiana to install a fluorescent system.

The Saturday after Thanksgiving, dozens of floats, vehicles, bands, marchers, and Santa Claus parade through the city's main streets to officially kick off the Christmas holiday season. Here, Helen Carroll rides in her convertible-turned-bed in the 1978 parade, themed "The Spirit of Christmas." (Jill Carroll.)

Every last weekend in July since 1998, Frankfort has closed off the streets surrounding the courthouse and celebrated its Hot Dog Festival, attracting thousands of visitors from throughout Indiana and surrounding states. Among the events are a parade, the 5-K Bun Run, a dachshund race, a hot dog eating contest, entertainment with dancing in the streets, and, of course, hot dogs with all the toppings. (Jill Carroll.)

Hollywood film crews, executives, and actors took over Frankfort for a week during the summer of 1992, when a major scene for the feature film *Blue Chips* was shot in Case Arena, above. The film, starring Nick Nolte and directed by William Friedkin, cast hundreds of area residents as spectators for the championship basketball game. The photograph below was taken in July 1993 at a dinner held at the Frankfort Country Club to honor the movie's executives and stars. The sheet cake, decorated by Frankfort's Marvel Albitz, is admired by, from left to right, William Friedkin, director; Anthony C. Hall, actor; Michele Rappaport, producer; J.T. Walsh, actor; and Ron Shelton, executive producer/screenwriter. Rossville designers Roz Eiler and Sue Rodkey created the Dolphin logo on the cake and T-shirts. (Above, Dick Withrow; below, Neil Conner.)

BIBLIOGRAPHY

61st General Assembly of Indiana. *Record of Indiana Volunteers in the Spanish-American War 1898–1899*. Indianapolis: Wm. B. Burford, Contractor for State Printing and Binding, 1900.

A Portrait and Biographical Record of Boone and Clinton Counties, Ind., Containing Biographical Sketches of Many Prominent and Representative Citizens. Chicago: A.W. Bowen & Co., 1895.

Claybaugh, Joseph. *History of Clinton County, Indiana*. Indianapolis: A.W. Bowen & Co., 1913.

Clinton County Bicentennial Committee. *Legacy, a Bicentennial Salute to Clinton County, Indiana*. Frankfort, IN: 1976.

Clinton County Centennial Committee. *A Century of Progress, an Account of the Clinton County Centennial with a General Review of the Past Century*. Frankfort, IN: 1930.

Clinton County Chamber of Commerce. *Celebrating Clinton County, a Community of Progress*. Frankfort, IN: 1988.

Clinton County Sesquicentennial Committee. *Clinton County Sesquicentennial 1830–1980*. Frankfort, IN: 1980.

Grove, Helen E. *Frankfort, A Pictorial History*. St. Louis, MO: G. Bradley Publishing Inc., 1992.

History of Clinton County, Indiana. Chicago: Inter-State Publishing Co., 1886.

www.genealogycenter.info

Information was also drawn from the Frankfort Community Public Library's microfilm, which contains the various Frankfort newspapers dating back to the late 1800s, including the following: *Frankfort Banner, Frankfort Crescent, Crescent-News, Frankfort News, Frankfort Weekly Times, Frankfort Evening Times, Frankfort Morning Times*, and *Frankfort Times*.

Visit us at
arcadiapublishing.com